Chelsea Kong

Biblical Puzzle Book
Volume 2

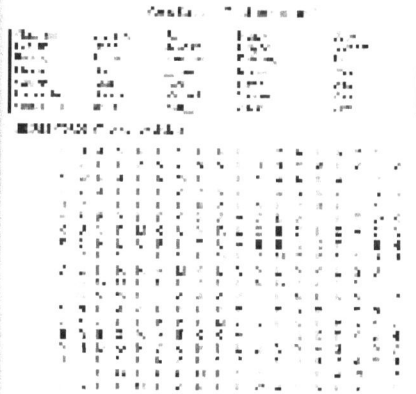

5 different types of puzzles
Bible stories included

Printed in 2021, Made in Toronto, Canada
ISBN: 978-1-7775168-1-9
Publisher: Self-Publish
Library and Archives Canada

Table of Contents

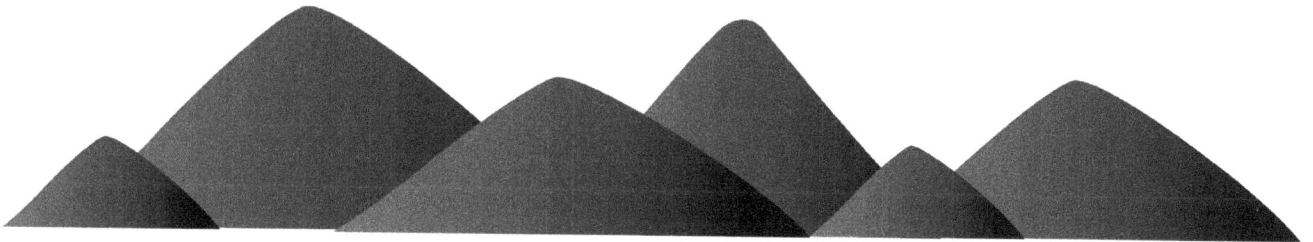

CROSSWORD PUZZLE – ESTHER

It is best to do from left to right for each word to solve the problem.

									13		14		
1	2		3										
									12				
				11									
			4										
						7							
			5		6								
											9		
						8							
										10			

Horizontal (Across)	Vertical (Down)
1 She was known as Hadassah (6 letters) *hint: King Ahasuerus married her 4 The king that showed favour to Esther (2 letters) *hint: Esther 1:1 5 The enemy of the Jews (5 letters) *hint: Esther 3:1 8 Esther was six months with oil of _____ (5 letters) *hint: Jesus was given this at his birth and by Mary (Esther 2:12) 10 Esther was purified with ____ of myrrh and six months with perfumes and cosmetics (3 letters) *hint: Esther 2:12 13 ?The king loved Esther above all the _____ (5 letters) * hint: Esther 2:17	2 The province of where King Ahasuerus lives (4 letters) *hint: His palace is there (Esther 1:2) 3 Mordecai raised her as his daughter (8 letters) *hint: Esther's real name (2 Chronicles 1:5) 6 Esther was six _____ with... (6 letters) *hint: Esther 2:12 7 The king sat on the throne of his _____ (5 letters) *hint: Esther 1:2 9 The queen that refused the king's request (6 letters) *hint: Esther 1:11 11 Esther said and her attendants would do this (4 letters) * hint: It is done for Passover 12 Esther's uncle who raised her as his daughter (9 letters) * hint: Haman wanted to hang him 14 Another word for king (7 letters) * hint: It expresses his greatness

Esther's Story

Esther 1

In those days of king Ahasuerus (Xerxes), which reigned from India and to Ethiopia, the king was having a feast in Shushan with the nobles and princes of the provinces. 4When he showed the riches of his glorious kingdom and the honour of his excellent majesty for many days, even a hundred and fourscore days later. It was the third year of his reign.

Queen Vashti was also having a feast with the women in the royal house, which belonged to the king. The king requested that the queen come before him to show her beauty. The queen refused to come and when they told the king then he became angry.

Esther 2:7

And he brought up Hadassah, that is Esther, his uncle's daughter: for she had neither father nor mother, and the maid was fair and beautiful; whom Mordecai when her father and mother were dead, took for his own daughter.

Esther 4:16

16 "Go, gather together all the Jews who are in Susa, and fast for me. Do not eat or drink for three days, night or day. I and my attendants will fast as you do. When this is done, I will go to the king, even though it is against the law. And if I perish, I perish."

Esther 5 (Esther's request to the king)

On the third day, Esther put on her royal robes and stood in the inner court of the palace, in front of the king's hall. The king was sitting on his royal throne in the hall, facing the entrance. 2 When he saw Queen Esther standing in the court, he was pleased with her and held out to her the gold scepter that was in his hand. So, Esther approached and touched the tip of the scepter.

Esther's Story continued...

Then the king asked, "What is it, Queen Esther? What is your request? Even up to half the kingdom, it will be given you."

"If it pleases the king," replied Esther, "let the king, together with Haman, come today to a banquet I have prepared for him."

"Bring Haman at once," the king said, "so that we may do what Esther asks." So, the king and Haman went to the banquet Esther had prepared. As they were drinking wine, the king again asked Esther, "Now what is your petition? It will be given to you. And what is your request? Even up to half the kingdom, it will be granted."

Esther replied, "My petition and my request is this: If the king regards me with favor and if it pleases the king to grant my petition and fulfill my request, let the king and Haman come tomorrow to the banquet I will prepare for them. Then I will answer the king's question."

Haman's anger against Mordecai
Haman went out that day happy and in high spirits. But when he saw Mordecai at the king's gate and observed that he neither rose nor showed fear in his presence, he was filled with rage against Mordecai. 10 Nevertheless, Haman restrained himself and went home.

He spoke to his wife Zeresh and his friends. He was happy about his wealth and his ten sons and all the ways that the king had honoured above all the nobles and officials. He was also very pleased that Queen Esther had invited him to a banquet with the king, but he was not content about Mordecai.

His wife and his friends told him to build gallows of seventy-five feet high and ask the king to hang Mordecai on in the morning. Haman liked the idea.

Esther's Story Continued...

Esther 6

That night the king was unable to sleep, so he ordered the book of chronicles is read to him, which is the record of his reign. There was a record of Bigthana and Teresh, two of the king's officers that wanted to assassinate him. He wanted to know if Mordecai was rewarded for this.

Then his attendants said, "Nothing was done for him."
"Who is in the court?" asked the king.

Haman just entered the outer court and the attendants told the king that Haman is in the outer court. He ordered them to bring him in.

Then the king asked Haman, "What should be done for the man that the king delights to honour?"

6Now Haman thought to himself, "Who is there that the king would rather honor than me?"

So he answered the king, "For the man the king delights to honor, 8have them bring a royal robe the king has worn and a horse the king has ridden, one with a royal crest placed on its head.

Then let the robe and horse be entrusted to one of the king's most noble princes. Let them robe the man the king delights to honor, and lead him on the horse through the city streets, proclaiming before him, 'This is what is done for the man the king delights to honor!'

"Go at once," the king commanded Haman. "Get the robe and the horse and do just as you have suggested for Mordecai the Jew, who sits at the king's gate. Do not neglect anything you have recommended."

Esther's Story Continued...

So Haman got the robe and the horse. He robed Mordecai, and led him on horseback through the city streets, proclaiming before him, "This is what is done for the man the king delights to honor!"

Afterward Mordecai returned to the king's gate. But Haman rushed home, with his head covered in grief, 13and told Zeresh his wife and all his friends everything that had happened to him. His advisers and his wife Zeresh said to him, "Since Mordecai, before whom your downfall has started, is of Jewish origin, you cannot stand against him-you will surely come to ruin!"

While they were still talking with him, the king's eunuchs arrived and hurried Haman away to the banquet Esther had prepared.

Esther 7

The King and Haman went to dine with Queen Esther. The king asked Queen Esther, "Queen Esther, what is your petition? It will be given you. What is your request? Even up to half the kingdom, it will be granted." Then Queen Esther answered, "If I have found favor with you, O king, and if it pleases your majesty, grant me my life-this is my petition. And spare my people-this is my request.

For I and my people have been sold for destruction and slaughter and annihilation. If we had merely been sold as male and female slaves, I would have kept quiet, because no such distress would justify disturbing the king.

King Xerxes asked Queen Esther, "Who is he? Where is the man who has dared to do such a thing?"

Esther's Story Continued...

Esther said, "The adversary and enemy is this vile Haman." Then Haman was terrified before the king and queen.

The king got up in a rage, left his wine and went out into the palace garden. But Haman, realizing that the king had already decided his fate, stayed behind to beg Queen Esther for his life.

Just as the king returned from the palace garden to the banquet hall, Haman was falling on the couch where Esther was reclining. The king exclaimed, "Will he even molest the queen while she is with me in the house?" As soon as the word left the king's mouth, they covered Haman's face.

Then Harbona, one of the eunuchs attending the king, said, "A gallows seventy-five feet high stands by Haman's house. He had it made for Mordecai, who spoke up to help the king." The king said, "Hang him on it!"

So they hanged Haman on the gallows he had prepared for Mordecai. Then the king's fury subsided.

CROSSWORD PUZZLE – Ezekiel

It is best to do from left to right for each word to solve the problem.

Horizontal (Across)	Vertical (Down)
2 The name of Ephraim and Manasseh's father (6 letters) *hint: Mary's husband (Ezekiel 37:16)	1 The nation that Ezekiel was to prophesy over (6 letters) *hint: smallest nation (Ezekiel 37:11)
3 The _____ of dry bones (6 letters) *hint: a deep area of land (Genesis 37:2)	5 The prophet who spoke over the dry bones (7 letters) *hint: the name of the puzzle
4 Man has _____ and skin (5 letters) * hint: Ezekiel 37:6	7 He spoke over the dry _____ and they became alive (5 letters) *hint: necessary to move the body
8 The _____ of the Lord (6 letters) *hint: Ezekiel 37:1	10 Ezekiel saw the valley and, they were very dry (9 letters) * hint: Ezekiel 37:2
9 Ezekiel received word from the _____ (4 letters) *hint: Ezekiel 37:1	11 _____ of man, can these bones live? (4 letters) *hint: (Ezekiel 37:3)
12 Ezekiel was told to _____ over the dry bones (8 letters) *hint: Ezekiel 37:4	

Ezekiel's Story

Ezekiel 37:1-7

Ezekiel was a prophet over Israel. The spirit of the Lord brought him to a valley which was full of bones. He saw that they were very dry.

The Lord said, "Son of man, can these bones live?"

Ezekiel answered, "O Lord God, you know."

And he said, "Prophesy to these bones, and say to them, O you dry bones, hear the word of the Lord."

The Lord said, "Behold, I will cause breath to enter into you, and you shall live. And I will lay sinews upon you, and will bring up flesh to you, and cover you with skin, and put breath in you, and ye shall live; and ye shall know that I am the Lord."

The Lord said, "Behold, I will cause breath to enter into you, and you shall live. And I will lay sinews upon you, and will bring up flesh to you, and cover you with skin, and put breath in you, and ye shall live; and ye shall know that I am the Lord."

So I prophesied as I was commanded: and as I prophesied, there was a noise, and behold a shaking, and the bones came together, bone to his bone. And when I saw the sinews and the flesh came up upon them, and the skin covered them above: but there was no breath in them.

Ezekiel 37:9-10

Then he said, "Prophesy to the wind, prophesy, son of man, and say to the wind, the Lord says; Come from the four winds, O breath, and breathe on these slain, that they may live."

So I prophesied as he commanded me, and the breath came into them, and they lived, and stood up on their feet, an exceeding and great army.

Ezekiel's Story

Ezekiel 37:16

"Son of man, take one stick, and write on it, for Judah, and for the children of Israel and his companions: then take another stick, and write on it, for Joseph, the stick of Ephraim and for all the house of Israel his companions."

CROSSWORD PUZZLE – Ezra

It is best to do from left to right for each word to solve the problem.

			1				8						
	2			3					10				
			4				9						
										11			
		5											
6							12						
7													
			13										
			14										

Horizontal (Across)	Vertical (Down)
[2] The king of Persia the Lord spoke about (6 letters) *hint: Jeremiah prophesied (Ezra 1:16)	[1] The one that serves in the temple (6 letters) *hint: He is must stay holy before God (Ezra 1:5)
[4] He is known as a scribe (4 letters) *hint: The story tells his name	[3] The one who records and writes letters for people (6 letters) *hint: Nehemiah 12:36
[6] Cyrus was told to _____ the house of the Lord (5 letters) * hint: Ezra 1:2	[5] The tribe of _____ means praise (5 letters) *hint: Jesus Christ was born into this tribe
[7] The Lord God of heaven has given Cyrus all the kingdoms of the _____ (5 letters) *hint: God created it for people	[8] The _____ are called to the work of the sanctuary (7 letters) *hint: tribe of the high priest and priests
[9] The nation of _____ is the smallest nation (6 letters) *hint: Ezra 1:3	[10] The _____ spoke to Cyrus (9 letters) * hint: He is the Creator
[14] Ezekiel received word from the _____ (4 letters) *hint: Ezekiel 37:1	[11] The tribe of _____ (8 letters) * hint: Ezra 1:5
	[12] The Lord created the _____ and earth (6 letters) * hint: His dwelling place
	[13] He is Sovereign (3 letters) *hint: (Ezra 1:3)

Ezra's Story

Ezra 1

In the first year of Cyrus, king of Persia, that the word of Lord by the mouth of Jeremiah might be fulfilled, the Lord stirred up the spirit of Cyrus king of Persia, that he had made a proclamation throughout all his kingdom, and put it also in writing, saying.

Cyrus king of Persia said, "The Lord God of heaven has given me all the kingdoms of the earth; and he has charged me to build him a house at Jerusalem, which is in Judah. Who is there among you of all his people? His God be with him, and let him go up to Jerusalem, which is in Judah, and build the house of the Lord God of Israel, (he is the God,) which is in Jerusalem.

And who ever remains in any place where he stays, let the men of his place help him with silver, and with gold, and with goods, and with beasts, besides the freewill offering for the house of God that is in Jerusalem."

Then the chief of the fathers of Judah and Benjamin, and the priests, and the Levites, with all them whose spirit of God had raised, to go up to build the house of the Lord which is in Jerusalem. And all of them were strengthened their hands with vessels of silver, with gold, with goods, and with beasts, and with precious things, beside all that was willingly offered.

Cyrus also brought vessels of the house of the Lord, which Nebuchadnezzar had brought out of Jerusalem, and had and put them into the house of the gods; Cyrus brought even those from Mithredath the treasurer, and counted them for Sheshbazzar, the prince of Judah. There were thirty chargers of gold, a thousand chargers of silver, twenty-nine knives, thirty basons of gold, silver basons of second sort four hundred and ten, and other vessels of gold and of silver were five thousand and four hundred. Sheshbazzar brought them all from Babylon to Jerusalem.

CROSSWORD PUZZLE - Jacob

The words connect with each other.

Horizontal (Across)	Vertical (Down)
1 The name of a place Jacob wrestled with God (6 letters) *hint: for I have seen God face to face, and my life is preserved (Genesis 32:30)	2 The name of Jacob's father (5 letters) *hint: His name means laughter
3 The one that Jacob kissed when he came to Haran (6 letters) *hint: Genesis 29:11	4 The place God lives (6 letters) *hint: Genesis 1:1
6 Isaac's wife _____ (7 letters) * hint: Laban's sister	5 Jacob was tricked by Laban to marry _____ (4 letters) *hint: Rachel's older sister
8 Abraham _____ the Lord (7 letters) *hint: Genesis 26:5	7 He is the king of Philistines (9 letters) * hint: Genesis 26:1
9 Abraham obeyed the _____ (4 letters) *hint: He counted Abraham as being righteous	9 The name of Jacob's brother (4 letters) *hint: He is a skilled hunter (Genesis 27:1)
10 His name means deceiver (5 letters) *hint: He deceived Esau to sell his birthright (Genesis 25:31)	11 Isaac _____ Jacob (7 letters) *hint: Genesis 27:27
12 The Lord promised to give the _____ of Canaan (4 letters) *hint: place to live	13 Jacob's uncle and Rebekkah's brother (5 letters) *hint: Genesis 26:12
14 Jacob's favourite son (7 letters) *hint: Rachel's first born son (Genesis 32:30)	15 Isaac _____ in the land, and received in the same year an hundredfold: and the Lord blessed him. (5 letters) *hint: Genesis 26:12

Jacob's Story Continued

Genesis 22:17-18
I will surely bless you and make your descendants as numerous as the stars in the sky and as the sand on the seashore. Your descendants will take possession of the cities of their enemies, and through your offspring all nations on earth will be blessed, because you have obeyed me."

Genesis 25:29-34
And Jacob sod pottage: and Esau came from the field, and he was faint; 30and Esau said to Jacob, 31Feed me, I pray thee, with that same red pottage; for I am faint: therefore was his name called Edom.
And Jacob said, "Sell me this day your birthright."
And Esau said, "Behold, I am at the point to die: and what profit shall this birthright to Jacob."
Then Jacob gave Esau bread and pottage of lentils; and he did eat and drink, and rose up, and went his way; this Esau despised his birthright.

Genesis 26:5
because Abraham obeyed me and kept my requirements, my commands, my decrees and my laws."

Genesis 26:8
When Isaac had been there a long time, Abimelech king of the Philistines looked down from a window and saw Isaac caressing his wife Rebekah.

Genesis 26:12
Isaac planted (sowed) crops in that land and the same year reaped a hundred-fold, because the Lord blessed him.

Jacob's Story continued...

Genesis 27:1-3

When Isaac was old and his eyes were so weak that he could no longer see, he called for Esau his older son and said to him, "My son." "Here I am," he answered.

Isaac said, "I am now an old man and don't know the day of my death. 3Now then, get your weapons-your quiver and bow-and go out to the open country to hunt some wild game for me. Prepare me the kind of tasty food I like and bring it to me to eat, so that I may give you my blessing before I die."

Genesis 27:27-29

So he went to him and kissed him. When Isaac caught the smell of his clothes, he blessed him and said, "Ah, the smell of my son is like the smell of a field that the Lord has blessed.

May God give you of heaven's dew and of earth's richness- an abundance of grain and new wine. May nations serve you and peoples bow down to you. Be lord over your brothers, and may the sons of your mother bow down to you. May those who curse you be cursed and those who bless you be blessed."

Genesis 27:33

Isaac trembled violently and said, "Who was it, then, that hunted game and brought it to me? I ate it just before you came and I blessed him-and indeed he will be blessed!"

Genesis 29:11

Then Jacob kissed Rachel and began to weep aloud. Rachel ran home to tell her father that Jacob had come and that she is the son of Rebekah. Jacob was welcomed into Laban's home.

Jacob's Story Continued

Genesis 29:16
Now Laban had two daughters; the name of the older was Leah, and the name of the younger was Rachel. Jacob was willing to work seven years to marry Rachel as his wife. Laban agreed to let him marry her. Leah was not very pretty, but Rachel was beautiful. Jacob was tricked into marrying Leah, but he also married Rachel, whom he loved. Jacob also received six sons and a daughter from Leah.

Rachel gave him Bilhah and she bore him two sons, Leah gave him Zilpah who bore him two sons, and Rachel then bore a son.

Genesis 30:25
She named him Joseph, and said, "May the Lord add to me another son." While Jacob was leaving Haran, he stayed alone and met a man and wrestled with him. He called that place Peniel because he saw God face to face, and his life is preserved. Later on, Rachel bore Jacob a second son and he called him, Benjamin. Rachel was dying in childbirth.

CROSSWORD PUZZLE - King Solomon

It is best to do from left to right for each word to solve the problem.

Horizontal (Across)	Vertical (Down)
2 Solomon said _____ be the Lord God of Israel (6 letters) *hint: 2 Chronicles 6:4	1 Solomon received _____ in an abundance (4 letters) *hint: precious metal (2 Chronicles 9:9)
4 A short word said in recognition of one's situation (2 letters) *hint: 1 Chronicles 21:23	3 Solomon asked the Lord for _____ (6 letters) *hint: He is known for this (2 Chronicles 1:5)
5 The Lord appeared to Solomon in a _____ (5 letters) *hint: 1 Kings 3:5	4 God _____ Israel to establish it (5 letters) *hint: 2 Chronicles 9:8
6 King David's son that became king (6 letters) *hint: He is the wisest king (2 Chronicles 9:1)	6 The queen of _____ visited King Solomon (5 letters) *hint: 2 Chronicles 9:1
8 The _____ of Sheba (4 letters) *hint: the wife of a king	8 The _____ are called to the work of the sanctuary (7 letters) *hint: tribe of the high priest and priests
9 Solomon _____ the temple (5 letters) * hint: 1 2 Chronicles 7:1	10 The _____ spoke to Cyrus (9 letters) * hint: He is the Creator
11 Then the _____ of the Lord filled the temple (5 letters) *hint: 2 Chronicles 7:1	11 The Lord is _____ in mercy (5 letters) * hint: 1 Kings 3:6
12 The Lord _____ to Solomon (8 letters) *hint: 1 Kings 3:5	

King Solomon's Story

2 Chronicles 6:4a
4Then he said: "Blessed be to the Lord, the God of Israel, who with his hands has fulfilled what he promised with his mouth to my father David."

2 Chronicles 7:1-2
When Solomon finished praying, fire came down from heaven and consumed the burnt offering and the sacrifices, and the glory of the Lord filled the temple. The priests could not enter the temple of the Lord because the glory of the Lord filled it.

2 Chronicles 9:1-2
And when the queen of Sheba heard of the fame of Solomon with hard questions at Jerusalem, with a very great company, and camels that bare spices, and gold in abundance, and precious stones; and when she came to Solomon, she communed with him about all that matters in her heart.

And Solomon told her all her questions: and there was nothing hidden from Solomon, which he didn't tell her. And when the queen of Sheba had seen the wisdom of Solomon, and the house that he had built, and 4the food on his table, the seating of his officials, the attending servants in their robes, the cupbearers in their robes and the burnt offerings he made at the temple of the Lord , she was overwhelmed.
She said to the king, "The report I heard in my own country about your achievements and your wisdom is true.

But I did not believe what they said until I came and saw with my own eyes. In-deed, not even half the greatness of your wisdom was told me; you have far exceeded the report I heard.

King Solomon's Story Continued...

How happy your men must be! How happy your officials, who continually stand before you and hear your wisdom!

2 Chronicles 9:8
The queen of Sheba said, "Blessed be the Lord the God, which delighted in you to set you on his throne, to be king for the Lord your God; because your God loved Israel, to establish them forever, therefore made he you king over them, to do judgement and justice."

And she gave the king a hundred and twenty talents of gold, and of spices great abundance, and precious stones; neither was there any this much spice as what the queen of Sheba gave king Solomon.
And the servants also of Huram, and the servants of Solomon, which brought gold from Ophir, brought gold from Ophir, brought algum trees and precious stones.

1 Kings 3:5-9
In Gibeon the Lord appeared to Solomon in a dream by night and God sad, "Ask what I will give you."

And Solomon said, "You have showed your servant David my father great mercy, according as he walked before you in truth, and in righteousness, and in uprightness of heart with you; and you have kept for him great kindness, that you have given him a son to sit on this throne, this day.

And now, O Lord my God, you have made your servant king instead of David my father; and I am but a little child: I do not know how to go out or come in. And your servant is in the midst of your people, which you have chosen, a great people, that can't be numbered or counted.

King Solomon's Story Continued...

Give your servant an understanding heart (wisdom) to judge your people; that I may discern between good and bad; for who is able to judge this people."

FILL-IN PUZZLE - Deuteronomy Blessings

The words connect with each other.

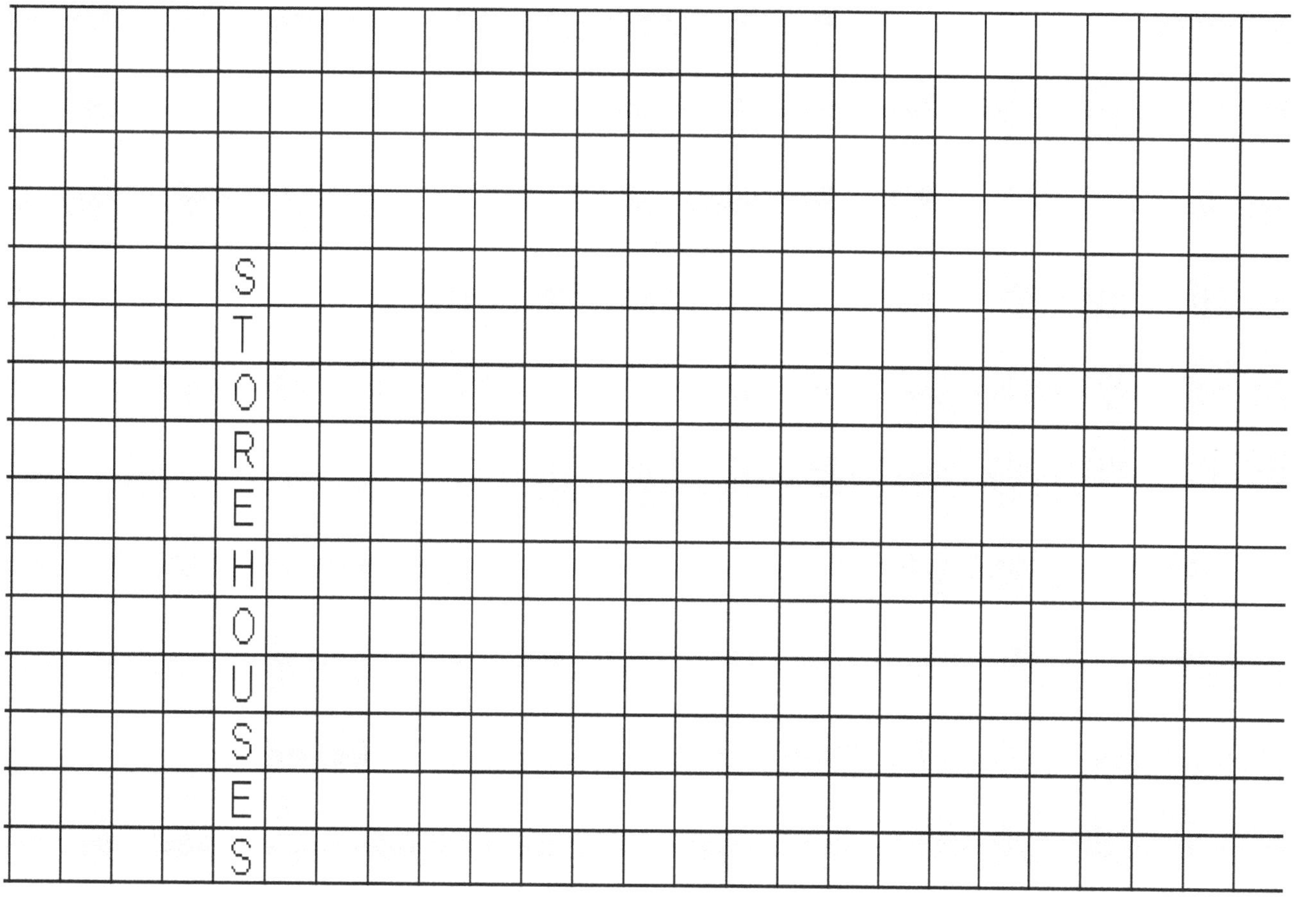

Vertical (Down)		Horizontal (Across)	
Above	Nations	Blessed	Land
Basket	Open	Blessings	Plenty
Day	Overtake	Establish	Voice
Field	Rain	Goods	Work
Hearken	Storehouses	Ground	
High		Head	
Houses		Heaven	
		Holy	
		Kine	

Deuteronomy Blessings

Deuteronomy 28

If you fully obey the Lord your God and carefully follow all his commands I give you today, the Lord your God will set you high above all the nations on earth. All these blessings will come upon you and accompany you if you obey the Lord your God: You will be blessed in the city and blessed in the country. The fruit of your womb will be blessed, and the crops of your land and the young of your livestock-the calves of your herds and the lambs of your flocks. Your basket and your kneading trough will be blessed. You will be blessed when you come in and blessed when you go out. The Lord will grant that the enemies who rise up against you will be defeated before you. They will come at you from one direction but flee from you in seven. 8The Lord will send a blessing on your barns and on everything you put your hand to. The Lord your God will bless you in the land he is giving you. The Lord will establish you as his holy people, as he promised you on oath, if you keep the commands of the Lord your God and walk in his ways.

Then all the peoples on earth will see that you are called by the name of the Lord, and they will fear you.

The Lord will grant you abundant prosperity-in the fruit of your womb, the young of your livestock and the crops of your ground-in the land he swore to your
forefathers to give you.

The Lord will open the heavens, the storehouse of his bounty, to send rain on your land in season and to bless all the work of your hands. You will lend to many nations but will borrow from none.

The Lord will make you the head, not the tail. If you pay attention to the commands of the Lord your God that I give you this day and carefully follow them, you will always be at the top, never at the bottom.

FILL-IN PUZZLE- David

The words connect with each other.

						M																			
						E																			
						P																			
						H																			
						I																			
						B																			
						O																			
						S																			
						H																			
						E																			
						T																			
						H																			

Vertical (Down)		Horizontal (Across)	
Abishai	Mephibosheth	Abiathar	Linen
Ahithophel	Seer	Absalom	Mouth
Amnon	Solomon	Banished	Night
Ark	Tamar	Bathsheba	Priests
Hushai	Zeruiah	David	Proverbs
Inheritance	Ziba	Fair	Reaches
Joab		Israel	Ruby
Jonadab		Ittai	Servant
King		Kingdom	Zadok
Lord		Nathan	

2 Samuel 13

Absalom the son of David had a fair sister, whose name was Tamar: and Amnon the son of David loved her. Amnon was so desirous for Tamar that he became sick. His friend was Jonadab, which is the son of Shimeah, David's brother.

King David's Story Continued...

Amnon listened to his friend's advice and asked for Tamar, but he abused her and hated her. Tamar did not marry because of this.

2 Samuel 14

King David knew about it and was very angry. Absalom hated Amnon for what he did. He waited two years before he tried to find a way to ask the king to join him and the other princes to Baalhazor for the sheepshearers were there. Then King David refused his request. Absalom asked him if Amnon could join him. The king asked him why, but Absalom kept pressing him to let Amnon go. Then he took this chance to have his servants kill Amnon.

The king's sons ran off and some of the servants came and told the king what Absalom had done. King David tore his garments and laid on the earth and all his servants did the same. Then Jonadab told King David that only Amnon was slain and not the rest of the sons because Absalom had planned this since the day Tamar was abused by him. Absalom ran away.

The kings' sons returned back crying. Absalom ran away to Talmai, the son of Ammihud the king of Geshur. He stayed there for three years. David mourned for the loss of Amnon.

Joab the son of Zeruiah noticed that the king desired Absalom. Joab got a wise woman from Tekoah to speak to the king. He told her what to tell the king. She did as he asked. She fell on her face to the ground and honoured David and asked for his help. She told him that she had two sons and they didn't get along with one another. Then one killed the other. The whole family has risen against her. She asked him to deliver the one that killed the other because they want to take his life and destroy the heir also. They will not leave any one left to keep her husband's name. She then told him to pardon and asked King David about his banished son.

King David's Story Continued...

He then knew that she was speaking about Absalom and asked if Joab had asked her to do so. He decided to have Absalom come back, but he refused to see him.

2 Samuel 15

Absalom sent spies out to the tribes of Israel and when they hear the trumpet sound they should say, "Absalom reigns in Hebron." He had two hundred men out of Jerusalem that were called and they went without knowing anything. Absalom sent Ahithophel the Gilonite, David's counsellor, from his city from Giloh, while he offered sacrifices. Then the plot against the king became strong, so the people supported Absalom. A messenger told David that the people's hearts are for Absalom, so David ordered his servants and everyone with him to leave quickly or evil may come against the city and people may die.

David had a servant named, Ittai and he was a stranger. He wanted to follow David, but he was told to go and stay in the palace, but he did not want to leave the king. David allowed him to stay with him. All the people cried as they left the city. Zadok and all the Levites were with him bearing the ark of the Covenant of God. And they set it down and Abiathar went up until all the people crossed over. The king told Zadok to carry the ark of God back into the city and hopes that favour may be granted to him to return safely back into the city. He told Zadok and his two sons, Ahimaz and Jonathan to return back to the city and to send him word when it is safe for him to return back. They did as he asked. David and his people continued along their way. He also prayed that the Lord would cause the counsel of Ahithophel to fail. Hushai the Archite came to meet him with coat rent and earth on his earth. David told him to return back to the palace and to serve in Absalom's presence and to defeat the counsel of Ahithophel. He said that he is a seer. He told him that Zadok, Abiathar, and the priests are there. He also told him that Ahimaz and Jonathan are also there.

King David's Story Continued...

2 Samuel 16

Ziba the servant of Mephibosheth met him with a couple of asses saddled, two hundred loaves of bread, a hundred summer fruits, and a bottle of wine. Shimei came and cursed as he came. He cursed against David. Abishai the son of Zeruiah wanted to kill him, but David would not allow him.

Fill-in PUZZLE - Proverbs 31 Woman

It is best to do from left to right for each word to solve the problem.

											E	X	C	E	L	L	E	S	T			

Vertical (Down)		Horizontal (Across)	
Blessed	Praise	Arise	Land
Call	Rejoice	Bread	Linen
Candle	Sells	Children	Mouth
Daughters	Spindle	Excellest	Night
Day	Truth	Favour	Proverbs
Girdles	Ways	Field	Reaches
Husband	Women	Fruit	Ruby
	Wool	Honour	Strength

Proverbs 31:10-31

Who can find a virtuous woman? For her price is far above rubies. The heart of her husband trusts safely in her, so that he will not have any need of spoil. She will do him good and not evil all the days of her life. She is a woman that knows how to seek wool, flax, and to work willingly with her hands. She is like the merchant's ships, which brings food from far away. She rises early while it is still night to pro-vide for her household and to give a portion of food to her maidens. She knows how to make decisions and to purchase a field. She plants a vineyard.

Proverbs 31 Woman's Story Continued...

She girds her loins with strength, and strengthens her arms. She perceives that her merchandise is good: her candle doesn't go out by night. She stretches her hand to help the poor and helps the needy. She is not afraid of the snow for her household, but she clothes them in scarlet.

She makes coverings of tapestry; her clothing is silk and purple. Her husband is known in the gates, when he sits among the elders of the land. She makes fine linen, and sells it; and delivers girdles to the merchant. Strength and honour are her clothing; and she shall rejoice in time to come. She opens her mouth with wisdom; and in her tongue is the law of kindness. She looks well after her household, and eats not the bread of idleness. Her children arise up, and call her blessed; her husband also, and he praises her. Many daughters have done virtuously, but you excellest them all. Favour is deceitful, and beauty is vain; but a woman that fears the Lord, she will be praised. Give her of the fruit of her hands; and let her own works praise her in the gates.

Fill-in PUZZLE - Malachi

It is best to do from left to right for each word to solve the problem.

	C	O	V	E	N	A	N	T										

Vertical (Down)		Horizontal (Across)	
Blessed	Return	Almighty	Judah
Change	Room	Ancestors	Kept
Fire	Seek	Ask	Me
Gold	Soap	Break	Robbing
Malachi	Stand	Covenant	Send
Purifier	Temple	Fruit	Silver
Refiner	Test	His	Tithes

Malachi 3

"I will send my messenger, who will prepare the way before me. Then suddenly the Lord you are seeking will come to his temple; the messenger of the covenant, whom you desire, will come," says the LORD Almighty.

But who can endure the day of his coming? Who can stand when he appears? For he will be like a refiner's fire or a launderer's soap.

Malachi's Story Continued...

He will sit as a refiner and purifier of silver; he will purify the Levites and refine them like gold and silver. Then the LORD will have men who will bring offerings in righteousness, and the offerings of Judah and Jerusalem will be acceptable to the LORD, as in days gone by, as in former years.

"So I will come to put you on trial. I will be quick to testify against sorcerers, adulterers and perjurers, against those who defraud laborers of their wages, who oppress the widows and the fatherless, and deprive the foreigners among you of justice, but do not fear me," says the LORD Almighty.

"I the LORD do not change. So you, the descendants of Jacob, are not destroyed. Ever since the time of your ancestors you have turned away from my decrees and have not kept them. Return to me, and I will return to you," says the LORD Almighty.
"But you ask, 'How are we to return?'

"Will a mere mortal rob God? Yet you rob me.

"But you ask, 'How are we robbing you?'
"In tithes and offerings. You are under a curse—your whole nation—because you are robbing me. Bring the whole tithe into the storehouse, that there may be food in my house. Test me in this," says the LORD Almighty, "and see if I will not throw open the floodgates of heaven and pour out so much blessing that there will not be room enough to store it. I will prevent pests from devouring your crops, and the vines in your fields will not drop their fruit before it is ripe," says the LORD Almighty. "Then all the nations will call you blessed, for yours will be a delightful land," says the LORD Almighty.

Fill-in PUZZLE - Revelation

It is best to do from left to right for each word to solve the problem.

								C	H	R	Y	S	O	L	Y	T	E		

Vertical (Down)		Horizontal (Across)	
Blessed	Praise	Arise	Land
Call	Rejoice	Bread	Linen
Candle	Sells	Children	Mouth
Daughters	Spindle	Excellest	Night
Day	Truth	Favour	Proverbs
Girdles	Ways	Field	Reaches
Husband	Women	Fruit	Ruby
	Wool	Honour	Strength

Revelation 21

John received a vision from the Lord. He saw a new heaven and a new earth because the first heaven and first earth had passed away and there was no more sea. "John saw the holy city, new Jerusalem, coming down from God out of heaven, prepared as a bride adorned for her husband" (Revelation 22:2).

Revelation Story Continued...

He heard a great voice out of heaven saying, Behold, the tabernacle of God is with men, and he will dwell with them, and they shall be his people, and God himself shall be with them, and be their God.

And I heard a great voice of heaven saying, Behold, the tabernacle of God is with men, and he will dwell with them, and they shall be his people, and God himself will be with them, and be their God. And God will wipe away all tears from their eyes; and there will be no more death, neither sorrow, nor crying, neither will there be any more pain; for the former things are passed away. And he that sat upon the throne said, Behold, I make all things new. And he said to me, Write these words are truth and faithful."

And he said to me, It is done. I am Alpha and Omega, the beginning and the end. I will give to him that is thirsty of the fountain of the water of life freely. He that overcomes will inherit all things; and I will be His God, and He will be my son. But the fearful, and unbelieving, and the tabernacle, and murderers, and whoremongers, and sorcerers, and idolaters, and all liars, will have their part in the lake which burns with fire and brimstone; which is the second death.

And there came to me one of the seven angels which had the seven vials full of the seven last plagues, and talked with me, saying, "Come here, I will show you the bride, the Lamb's wife." And he carried me away in the spirit to a great and high mountain and showed me that great city, the holy Jerusalem, descending out of heaven from God. Having the glory of God, and her light was like a stone most precious, even like a jasper stone, clear as crystal.

It had a great, high wall with twelve gates, and with twelve angels at the gates. On the gates were written the names of the twelve tribes of Israel.

Revelation Story Continued...

There were three gates on the east, three on the north, three on the south and three on the west. The wall of the city had twelve foundations, and on them were the names of the twelve apostles of the Lamb. The angel who talked with me had a measuring rod of gold to measure the city, its gates and its walls.

The city was laid out like a square, as long as it was wide. He measured the city with the rod and found it to be 12,000 stadia in length, and as wide and high as it is long.

He measured its wall and it was 144 cubits thick, by man's measurement, which the angel was using.

The wall was made of jasper, and the city of pure gold, as pure as glass. 19The foundations of the city walls were decorated with every kind of pre-cious stone. The first foundation was jasper, the second sapphire, the third chalcedony, the fourth emerald, the fifth sardonyx, the sixth carnelian, the seventh chrysolyte, the eighth beryl, the ninth topaz, the tenth chrysoprase, the eleventh jacinth, and the twelfth amethyst. The twelve gates were twelve pearls, each gate made of a single pearl. The great street of the city was of pure gold, like transparent glass.
I did not see a temple in the city, because the Lord God Almighty and the Lamb are its temple.
The city does not need the sun or the moon to shine on it, for the glory of God gives it light, and the Lamb is its lamp. The nations will walk by its light, and the kings of the earth will bring their splendor into it. On no day will its gates ever be shut, for there will be no night there. The glory and honor of the na-tions will be brought into it. Nothing impure will ever enter it, nor will anyone who does what is shameful or deceitful, but only those whose names are writ-ten in the Lamb's book of life.

Revelation Story Continued...

Revelation 22
Then the angel showed me the river of the water of life, as clear as crys-tal, flowing from the throne of God and of the Lamb down the middle of the great street of the city. On each side of the river stood the tree of life, bearing twelve crops of fruit, yielding its fruit every month. And the leaves of the tree are for the healing of the nations.

But he said to me, "Do not do it! I am a fellow servant with you and with your brothers the prophets and of all who keep the words of this book. Wor-ship God!" Let him who does wrong continue to do wrong; let him who is vile con-tinue to be vile; let him who does right continue to do right; and let him who is holy continue to be holy."

I am the Alpha and the Omega, the First and the Last, the Beginning and the End. And if anyone takes words away from this book of prophecy, God will take away from him his share in the tree of life and in the holy city, which are described in this book.

SCRAMBLED PUZZLE– Abraham

The words connect with each other.

Rmbaa	Olt
Mrabaha	Tinoans
Elsbs	Nlnpia
Anacan	Ohrapaoh
Altcte	Ertophp
Eontvcna	Cirh
Gtpye	Raisa
Tiafh	Arash
Vgie	Eesd
Dgo	Enett
Ergta	Aklw
Dnal	
Rodl	

Abram and his wife Sarai came to Egypt. Sarai was fair looking woman. Then Abram told Sarai to claim that she is his sister because he was afraid of Pharaoh. The Lord plagued Pharaoh's house because of Sarai. Pharaoh asked Abraham about this and then he told him that Sarai is his wife. He saw Abram as a prophet. Then he sent them away. Lot was with him and Abram was great in wealth and substance. There was a strife because the herdsmen because there wasn't enough land. Abram told Lot let there be no strife between them. He let Lot choose the land that he wanted and Abram took the rest. Lot chose the land that faced Sodom and Gomorrah.

Abraham's Story Continued...

The Lord told to walk the land and it will be his and belong to his descendants to come. He also told Abraham to count the stars and this will be how many descendants he would have. He believed God and it was counted to his as righteousness.

Abram saved Lot from Chedorlaomer and the kings that were with him. The King of Sodom went to meet Abram. He wanted to take the people and give Abram the goods, but Abram said he wanted nothing. He wanted the men to have what they wanted, but he would not allow the King of Sodom to claim that he made Abram rich. Melchizedek met Abram and came with bread and wine. Then Abram gave him a tenth of all that he had.

God made a covenant with Abram and called in Abraham, which means father of many nations. Sarai was to be named, Sarah, which means the mother of many nations. He promised Abram that if he walked perfect before him, he would fulfill His covenant with him. God would make Abram exceedingly fruitful, and he will make nations of him, and kings shall come out of him. He will establish his covenant between him and Abram and to his seed to come and in their generations an everlasting covenant to be a God to them and the seed after him. He will give to him and his seed to come the land of Canaan as an everlasting possession and he would be their God.

The Lord said, "That in blessing I will bless thee, and in multiplying I will multiply thy seed as the stars of the heaven, and as the sand which is upon the seashore; and thy seed shall possess the gate of his enemies; And in thy seed shall all the nations of the earth be blessed; because you have obeyed my voice."

SCRAMBLED PUZZLE- Isaiah

Mix the letters around. Read through the story.

Dehaa	Gnkis
Genal	Anld
Hzhaa	Eycrm
Lsabt	Edyaper
Lcaen	Vase
Yads	Icsk
Earhd	Uns
Zekehiah	Words
Aihasi	Emit
Audhj	Rstut
Eeramusjle	Iniosv
Dilekld	

Isaiah received a vision from God about **Judah** and **Jerusalem**. It was in the days of Uzziah, Jotham, **Ahaz**, and **Hezekiah**, which are the kings of Judah. The Lord told him that the people have disobeyed him. He told them to make themselves clean from all evil and not to do evil anymore.

In the time of Hezekiah when he was king of Judah, Isaiah told him not be afraid of the words of his enemy because he spoke evil against the Lord. The Lord would send a blast upon him and he will hear a rumour, and return to his own land. Then he will be killed by the sword. When Rabshekah returned to his land, he found out that the king of Assyria was fighting against Libnah. He heard that he had left. He heard that there was war in Ethiopia and told

Abraham's Story Continued...

Hezekiah not to trust in God to save them from his hand.

The Lord was with Hezekiah and sent an angel to the camp of the Assyrians and killed them all. Sennacherib ran away and stayed in Nineveh. He was worshipping his god and then his two sons killed him and escaped. His other son was made king in his place.

One day when Hezekiah was sick, Isaiah came to warn him that he has to get his house in order and prepare to die. Hezekiah **prayed** to God for **mercy** and reminded him of all the things he did right.

Then God heard him and had mercy on him. He told Isaiah to go back to Hezekiah. Isaiah asked if it is easier for the Lord to make the move ahead or backwards in time. He said that it is harder to move time backwards. Then Isaiah told him that the Lord is granting him 15 years more to live. He was well again.

SCRAMBLED PUZZLE- Job

Mix the letters around. Read through the story.

essas	Rold
Adbdil	Rceptfe
Dslsebe	Yrepad
Osbli	Asant
Lmceas	Evnse
Uetshdgar	Satnvsre
Elihu	Eheps
Eliphaz	Noss
Iaeftrs	Herte
Odg	Xneo
Ojb	Fwei
Vdivle	Aporzh

Job 1

In the land of Uz there lived a man whose name was Job. This man was blame less and upright; he feared God and shunned evil. He had seven sons and three daughters, and he owned seven thousand sheep, three thousand camels, five hundred yoke of oxen and five hundred donkeys, and had a large number of servants. He was the greatest man among all the people of the East.

Job's Story Continued...

His sons used to hold feasts in their homes on their birthdays, and they would invite their three sisters to eat and drink with them. When a period of feasting had run its course, Job would make arrangements for them to be purified.

Early in the morning he would sacrifice a burnt offering for each of them, thinking, "Perhaps my children have sinned and cursed God in their hearts." This was Job's regular custom.

One day the angels came to present themselves before the Lord, and Satan also came with them. The Lord said to Satan, "Where have you come from?"

Satan answered the Lord, "From roaming throughout the earth, going back and forth on it." Then the Lord said to Satan, "Have you considered my servant Job? There is no one on earth like him; he is blameless and upright, a man who fears God and shuns evil."

"Does Job fear God for nothing?" Satan replied. "Have you not put a hedge around him and his household and everything he has? You have blessed the work of his hands, so that his flocks and herds are spread throughout the land. But now stretch out your hand and strike every-thing he has, and he will surely curse you to your face."

The Lord said to Satan, "Very well, then, everything he has is in your power, but on the man, himself do not lay a finger."

Then Satan went out from the presence of the Lord.

One day when Job's sons and daughters were feasting and drinking wine at the oldest brother's house, a messenger came to Job and said, "The oxen were plowing and the donkeys were grazing nearby, and the Sabeans attacked and made off with them. They put the servants to the sword, and I am the only one who has escaped to tell you!"

While he was still speaking, another messenger came and said, "The fire of God fell from the heavens and burned up the sheep and the servants, and I am the only one who has escaped to tell you!"

Job's Story Continued...

While he was still speaking, another messenger came and said, "The Chaldeans formed three raiding parties and swept down on your camels and made off with them. They put the servants to the sword, and I am the only one who has escaped to tell you!"

While he was still speaking, yet another messenger came and said, "Your sons and daughters were feasting and drinking wine at the oldest brother's house, when suddenly a mighty wind swept in from the desert and struck the four corners of the house. It collapsed on them and they are dead, and I am the only one who has escaped to tell you!"

At this, Job got up and tore his robe and shaved his head. Then he fell to the ground in worship and said:

"Naked I came from my mother's womb,
    and naked I will depart.
The Lord gave and the Lord has taken away;
    may the name of the Lord be praised."

In all this, Job did not sin by charging God with wrongdoing.

SCRAMBLED PUZZLE - Joel

Mix the letters around. Read through the story.

Olbw	Aiunotmn
Lecnase	Atnoin
Orcn	loi
YCr	Etpuhel
Asft	Ortnsg
Eifr	Atrsr
Oejl	Uns
Aenvhe	Rupmtet
Lyoh	Awr
Erhsos	Eiwn
Nilo	Eivn
Oomn	Nizo

Joel's Story

The Lord spoke to **Joel** the son of **Pethuel**. He was called to give warning to the nation of Israel of what is to come. He told them that a nation is coming upon the land, strong, and without number, whose teeth are the teeth of a lion, and he has the cheek teeth of a great lion.

He had made the vine wasted and made the fig tree bare. He has cast away the branches, so that they have become white. He told the people to cry out in rags for the husband of their youth. The priests would mourn because of the meat offering and drink offering would be cut off. There was a warning for every person.

He also spoke about a fast to the Lord. All the people must join it and cry out to the Lord. The Lord would come and destroy them if they don't change. He told the priests to blow the trumpet in Zion and sound an alarm in the Lord's holy mountain.

The day of the Lord is coming near. It is a day of darkness and of gloom as the morning spread over the mountains. A great people and strong like none other. There will none like them in the many years of the generations to come. A fire will devour before them and behind them a flame burns the land like the garden of Eden ahead of them and the wilderness is behind them. Nothing is able to escape them. They appear to look like horses and horsemen. They will run. They will make the sound of fire that devours the stubble like a strong people ready for battle. They will be mighty men and be like men in war. They will run and enter into the windows like a thief. The earth will quake before them; the heavens will shake; the sun and the moon will be dark, and the stars will stop shining. The Lord will speak to command this army. It will be a great and terrible day.

Joel's Story

The people must gather together and **cleanse** themselves. They must be prepared for the bridegroom. The priests are to cry out at the altar to ask God to have mercy on the people. Then he will have mercy on them and send them corn, wine, and oil. The people will be satisfied.

SCRAMBLED PUZZLE - Habakkuk

Mix the letters around. Read through the story.

Agele	Orpud
Ate	Unr
Itafh	Asw
Lfy	Ese
Arget	Losu
Aakbuhkak	Paesk
Usjt	Tnasd
Eivl	Ablet
Arcmh	Owret
Atnsoni	Aiwt
Alipn	Atcwh
Ertpeph	Eriwt

Habakkuk's Story

Habakkuk the prophet saw visions from the Lord. He saw the Chaldeans march through the land to possess and dwell there. They are terrible and dreadful; their judgement and their dignity will proceed of themselves. Their horses also are swifter than the leopards, and are fiercer than the evening wolves; and their horsemen shall come from far; they will fly as the eagle that is in a hurry to eat.

Habakkuk said, "I stand upon my watch, and set me upon the tower, and will watch to see what
he will say to me, and what I will answer when I am reproved."

The Lord answered, "Write the vision, and make it plain on tables, that he may run that reads it. For the vision is yet for an appointed time, but at the end it shall speak, and not lie: though it tarry, wait for it; because it will surely come, it will not wait. The soul which is lifted up is not upright; but the just will live by his faith. The man that doesn't live by faith sins and he is a proud man. He doesn't stay at home and he makes his desire for hell and death great. He can't be satisfied, but gathers all nations and heaps all the people."

WORD MATCH PUZZLE– Gideon

Mix the letters around. Read through the story.

Face to Face with God	Angel
False God the men of Abiezer worshipped	Baal
Gideon's father	Egypt
Gideon's army he brought to Phurah	Gideon
He visited Gideon	Israel
Mighty man of valour	Lord
The children of Israel were brought out of	Midianites
The enemies that the Lord delivered the Israelites	Jehovah-Shalom
The name of the altar built to the Lord	Joash
The people the Lord brought out of Egypt	The people of Abiezer
They wanted to kill Gideon	Three hundred men

Judges 6

The children of Israel did evil in God's sight, so he delivered them to the Midianites for seven years. When the people sowed in the land, their enemies came and destroyed all that they had and left nothing for them. They cried to God and he sent a prophet to remind them that they were brought out of Egypt and from bondage. He gave them their land. The Lord told His people that He is their Lord and told them not the be afraid of the Amorites, but they did not obey.

An angel came and visited Gideon and called him a mighty man of valour. He told him that the Lord has left them and delivered them into the hands of the Midianites. The Lord told him that he would save Israel. Gideon told the Lord that he is from a poor family and he is the least of them. God promised him that he is with him and will smite the Midianites. Gideon asked the Lord to show him a sign. The Lord told him to bring him a present and he would wait for him. Gideon prepared a kid, unleavened cakes of ephah of flour and put the meat into a basket. He brought the broth in a pot. He gave it to the Lord.

Gideon's Story Continued...

The angel of the Lord touched the end of the staff that was in his hand, and touched the cakes, arose from the fire out of the rock, and consumed the flesh and unleavened cakes.

The angel left after that. Gideon perceived that it is an angel. He realized that he met God face to face. The Lord told him not be afraid and that he won't die. Then he built an altar to the Lord and called it Jehovah-Shalom. It is located in Ophrah and Abiezrites even now. That same night the Lord asked him to take his father's young second bullock, which was 7 years old and to throw down

the altar of Baal that his father has and cut down the grove by it. He built an altar there and sacrificed the bullock as a burnt sacrifice with wood from the grove he cut down. Gideon had seven servants with him to fulfill the task. He did it at night because he was afraid of his father's household and the men of the city.

Then asked his father, Joash who had done this and they found out that it was Gideon. They wanted to kill him. He asked them will they plead for Baal. If he is a god, then he can defend himself. The Spirit of the Lord came on Gideon and he blew the trumpet and the people of Abeizer followed after him. He sent messengers in Manasseh who also gathered after him, those of Asher, Zebulun, and Naphtali. He told God that he would save Israel as God told him. Then the Lord told him that he would put a fleece of wool on the ground and if the dew is only in the fleece then he would know that God will save Israel. God fulfilled this and then Gideon asked him to have the dew fill the ground, but the fleece of wool to be dry. God fulfilled his request and he believed him.

Gideon's Story Continued...

Judges 7

Gideon had three two thousand men with him, but the Lord told him that there were too many. God told him to send those who are fearful back to their homes, so twenty-two thousand left and ten thousand remained. God told Gideon that there are still too many men. He told Gideon to tell the people to come down to the water. Those that drink the water with his tongue like a dog must be separated from those who bow and knew on their knees. There were three hundred men that lapped and put their hand to their mouth. The other people bowed and kneeled down. Gideon was told to keep the three hundred men and send the rest home. He told the rest of the people to return to their tents to rest.

They took victuals in their hand, and their trumpets. The Lord told Gideon to go down to the host and he has delivered them into his hand. He told Gideon that he was afraid that he should go to the enemy's camp with Phurah, which is his servant.

The Midianites and Amalekites were gathered together. They appeared like grasshoppers. A man told them about his dream that he saw a cake of barley bread tumbled into the host of Midian and came to a tent and hit it and it fell. It overturned and lay along. They realized that this is Gideon and that he has victory over them. Then Gideon believed God's word.

WORD MATCH PUZZLE– Samuel

Mix the letters around. Read through the story.

Face to Face with God	Angel
False God the men of Abiezer worshipped	Baal
Gideon's father	Egypt
Gideon's army he brought to Phurah	Gideon
He visited Gideon	Israel
Mighty man of valour	Lord
The children of Israel were brought out of	Midianites
The enemies that the Lord delivered the Israelites	Jehovah-Shalom
The name of the altar built to the Lord	Joash
The people the Lord brought out of Egypt	The people of Abiezer
They wanted to kill Gideon	Three hundred men

1 Samuel 1

A man named, Elkanah had two wives; Hannah and Peninnah. Peninnah had children, but Hannah had none. He went to the city every year to worship and sacrifice to the Lord in Shiloh. Eli's two sons, Hophni and Phinehas the priests were there. When it came to his time to offer sacrifices, he also gave Peninnah's sons and daughters their portions. He gave Hannah a worthy portion because he loved her, but the Lord had not given her children. Her adversary kept speaking against her because she had no children. She finally decided that she would not eat.

Elkanah asked Hannah why she is crying and would not eat. He questioned her, "Am I not better than ten sons?" She rose up after she had eaten and drunk in Shiloh. She went to the temple and Eli the priest sat by the post of the temple of the Lord. Hannah was bitter in her soul and prayed to the Lord and cried. She made a vow to God that if He would look on the affliction of his handmaid and remember her, but to give her a man child, then she would give him the Lord all the days of his life and no razor would come on his head. During the time she was praying, Eli saw her. She was spoke in her heart and her lips moved, but there was no sound. He told she was drunk.

Samuel's Story Continued...

He asked her how long she had been drinking and to put away her wine. She told him, "No, my lord, I am a woman of sorrowful spirit. I have drunk neither wine nor strong drink, but have poured out my soul before the Lord. Count not your handmaid to be a daughter of Belial (a group of people who do evil): for out of the abundance of my complaint and grief have I spoken."

Then Eli said, "Go in peace: and the God of Israel grant you your petition that you have asked of him."

And she said, "Let your handmaid find grace in your sight."

Then she went away and ate and was no longer sad. Elkanah, Penninah and her children, and Hannah worshipped the Lord before they went back to Ramah. The Lord remembered Hannah and when the time was right she gave birth to a son and called him, Samuel. His name mean, "Because I have asked him of the Lord."

Elkanah went for the yearly sacrifice and his vow, but Hannah didn't go because she wanted to wait until the child was weaned and then she would bring him that he may appear before the Lord and abide there forever.

Elkanah told her, "Do what seems good to you and stay until you have weaned him. May the Lord establish His word."

She looked after Samuel until she had weaned him. When she had weaned him, then she took him with her along with three bullocks, one ephah of flour, and a bottle of wine. She brought them to the house of the Lord in Shiloh and the child was young. They killed a bullock and brought the child to Eli.

She told Eli, "Oh, my lord, as your soul lives, my lord. I am the woman that stood by you here, praying to the Lord. This child is what I prayed for and the Lord has given me my petition. I have also lent him to the Lord as long as he lives, he will be lent to the Lord. And he worshipped the Lord there."

1 Samuel 2
Hannah rejoiced to the Lord. Samuel ministered before the Lord as a child and wore a linen ephod. Hannah made him a little coat and brought it to him every year when she came with her husband for the yearly sacrifice.

Samuel's Story Continued...

Eli blessed Elkanah and Hannah and said, "The Lord give you seed of this woman for the loan which is lent to the Lord."

I have drunk neither wine nor strong drink, but have poured out my soul before the Lord. Count not your handmaid to be a daughter of Belial (a group of people who do evil): for out of the abundance of my complaint and grief have I spoken."
Then Eli said, "Go in peace: and the God of Israel grant you your petition that you have asked of him."
And she said, "Let your handmaid find grace in your sight."

Then she went away and ate and was no longer sad. Elkanah, Penninah and her children, and Hannah worshipped the Lord before they went back to Ramah. The Lord remembered Hannah and when the time was right, she gave birth to a son and called him, Samuel. His name means, "Because I have asked him of the Lord."

Elkanah went for the yearly sacrifice and his vow, but Hannah didn't go because she wanted to wait until the child was weaned and then she would bring him that he may appear before the Lord and abide there forever.

Elkanah told her, "Do what seems good to you and stay until you have weaned him. May the Lord establish His word."

She looked after Samuel until she had weaned him. When she had weaned him, then she took him with her along with three bullocks, one ephah of flour, and a bottle of wine. She brought them to the house of the Lord in Shiloh and the child was young. They killed a bullock and brought the child to Eli.

She told Eli, "Oh, my lord, as your soul lives, my lord. I am the woman that stood by you here, praying to the Lord. This child is what I prayed for and the Lord has given me my petition. I have also lent him to the Lord as long as he lives, he will be lent to the Lord. And he worshipped the Lord there."

Samuel's Story Continued...

1 Samuel 2

Hannah rejoiced to the Lord. Samuel ministered before the Lord as a child and wore a linen ephod. Hannah made him a little coat and brought it to him every year when she came with her husband for the yearly sacrifice.

Eli blessed Elkanah and Hannah and said, "The Lord give you seed of this woman for the loan which is lent to the Lord."

WORD MATCH PUZZLE– Jesus

Mix the letters around. Read through the story.

He asked Jesus to call him to walk on water	Disciples
He walked on the water	Faith
He was put in prison by Herod for Herodias	Five loaves and two fishes
Herodias daughter danced before him	Five thousand men
Jesus had this when He walked on water	Herod
Jesus is known to be	Jesus
The disciples found this much leftover	John the Baptist
The disciples gave Jesus to feed the multitude	Peter
They gave the bread and the fishes to Jesus	Son of God
The number of the multitude that heard Jesus	Twelve Baskets

Matthew 14

At this time, Herod knew about Jesus and he thought that he was John the Baptist raised from the dead because he had put him into prison for Herodias sake, his brother Philip's wife. John the Baptist told him that it is not lawful to marry his brother's wife. He wanted to put him to death, but he was afraid of the multitude because he considered him to be a prophet.

On his birthday, the daughter of Herodias danced them and he promised to give her whatever she asked of him. She was told by her mother ahead of time to bring John the Baptist head in a charger. The king was sorry and kept his oath. He had the head given to her and she brought it to her mother. His disciples came and took his body and buried it. They told Jesus about it.

Jesus left there and took a ship into the desert and the people heard and followed him on foot from the cities. Jesus went and saw a great multitude and he was moved with compassion. He healed their sick and when it became evening the disciples told him to send the multitude away. Jesus told them that they don't need to leave, but give them something to eat. They found a boy with a basket of five loaves and two fishes and brought it to Jesus. Then Jesus took it and blessed it. He gave it to his disciples and asked them to give it to the people to eat.

Jesus' Story Continued...

The people took from the basket and all five thousand men along with women and children ate and were full. In those days, the men and children were counted separately. Then Jesus instructed that the disciples gather the leftovers. They found twelve baskets full and brought it to Jesus.

Author's Comment:
This is often called the feeding of the 5000 and women and children are included into the number rather than separately. If we count it using our Math, it would be over 10,000 people. It has to be a miracle from God.

WORD MATCH PUZZLE- Joel

Mix the letters around. Read through the story.

Blow the trumpet in... He is gracious and merciful, slow to anger, and of great kindness, and repents him of the evil. The Lord promised to pour out this over all flesh He said to proclaim among these people; Prepare war, wake up mighty men of war, draw near; let them come up I will gather all the nations, and bring them down into the valley of... Ministers of the Lord The Lord said to these people, "Sanctify a fast..." The mountains shall drop down new wine... This place will dwell in Jerusalem forever	Children of Israel Gentiles Jehoshophat Jerusalem Joel Judah Lord Priests Spirit Zion

Joel 1:1-4

The word of the Lord that came to Joel was, "Hear this, you old men, and give ear, all you inhabitants of the land. Has this been in your days, or even in the days of your fathers? Tell your children of it, and let your children tell their children, and their children another generation. That which the cankerworm has left the locust has eaten; and that which the locust left the cankerworm has eaten; and that which the cankerworm has left the caterpillar has eaten."

Joel 1:14

Sanctify you a fast, call a solemn assembly, gather the elders, and all the inhabitants of the land into the house of the Lord your God, and cry to the Lord.

Joel 2:1

Blow the trumpet in Zion and sound an alarm in my holy mountain; let all the inhabitants of the land tremble; for the day of the Lord comes, for it is near at hand.

Joel's Story Continued...

Joel 2:13
And rend your heart, and not your garments, and turn to the Lord your God; for He is gracious and merciful, slow to anger, and of great kindness, and repents Him of the evil.

Joel 2:28
And it shall come to pass afterward, that I will pour out my spirit upon all flesh; and your sons and your daughters shall prophesy, your old men shall see visions; and also upon the servants and upon the handmaids in those days will I pour out my spirit.

Joel 3:2
I will gather all nations, and will bring them down into the valley of Jehoshaphat, and will plead with them there for my people and for my heritage Israel, who they have scattered among the nations, and parted my land.

Joel 3:9
Proclaim you this among the Gentiles; Prepare war, wake up the mighty men, let all the men of war draw near; let them come up;

Joel 3:18
And it shall come to pass in that day, that the mountains shall drop down new wine, and the hills that flow with milk, and all the rivers of Judah shall flow with waters, and a fountain shall come forth of the house of the Lord, and shall water the valley of Shittim.

Joel 3:20
But Judah shall dwell forever, and Jerusalem from generation to generation.

WORD MATCH PUZZLE– Ephesians

Mix the letters around. Read through the story.

Blow the trumpet in...	Children of Israel
He is gracious and merciful, slow to anger, and of great kindness, and repents him of the evil.	Gentiles
	Jehoshophat
The Lord promised to pour out this over all flesh	Jerusalem
He said to proclaim among these people; Prepare war, wake up mighty men of war, draw near; let them come up	Joel
	Judah
I will gather all the nations, and bring them down into the valley of...	Lord
	Priests
Ministers of the Lord	Spirit
The Lord said to these people, "Sanctify a fast..."	Zion
The mountains shall drop down new wine...	
This place will dwell in Jerusalem forever	

Ephesians 1:3, 5

Paul, an apostle of Christ Jesus by the will of God, To the saints in Ephesus, the faithful in Christ Jesus:

Grace and peace to you from God our Father and the Lord Jesus Christ.

Praise be to the God and Father of our Lord Jesus Christ, who has blessed us in the heavenly realms with every spiritual blessing in Christ.

5he predestined us to be adopted as his sons through Jesus Christ, in accordance with his pleasure and will--

Ephesians 1:17

I keep asking that the God of our Lord Jesus Christ, the glorious Father, may give you the Spirit of wisdom and revelation, so that you may know him better.

Ephesians' Story Continued...

Ephesians 4:11-12
It was he who gave some to be apostles, some to be prophets, some to be evangelists, and some to be pastors and teachers, to prepare God's people for works of service, so that the body of Christ may be built up...

Ephesians 1:20
built on the foundation of the apostles and prophets, with Christ Jesus himself as the chief cornerstone.

Ephesians 5:22
Wives, submit yourselves to your own husbands as to the Lord.

Ephesians 5:25
Husbands, love your wives, even as Christ also loved the church, and gave Himself for it;

Ephesians 6:1
Children, obey your parents in the Lord; for this is right. Honour your father and mother; (which is the first commandment with promise;)

Ephesians 6:11-17
Put on the whole armour of God, that you may be able to stand against the wiles of the devil. For we wrestle not against flesh and blood, but against principalities, against powers, against the rules of the darkness of this world, against spiritual wickedness in high places. Wherefore take to you the whole armour of, that you may be able to withstand in the evil day, and having done all, to stand. Stand therefore, having your loins girt about with truth, and having on the breastplace of righteousness; And your feet shod with the preparation of the gospel of peace; Above all, take the shield of faith, which you will be able to quench all the fiery darts of the wicked. And take the helmet of salvation, and the sword of the Spirit, which is the word of God.

WORD SEARCH PUZZLE– Peter

SECRET WORDS: (They can be obvious)

Abundance	Great	Light	Peace	Servant
Apostle	Heaven	Lord	Peter	Tabernacle
Christ	Holy	Majesty	Power	Truth
Divine	Honour	Multiplied	Precious	Wife
Faith	Jesus	Patience	Saviour	Virtue
Glory	Knowledge			Voice

```
E C N A D N U B A M J Y T S E J A M
K O E U T R I V H L D N O A U Z V R
N W G J F R O Y E I N R E W O P T Q
A Y R Q M I A P V C B Q L X G D A P
B P T B C B S I Z L M H P Y R O B A
M S O E V O N X O A G F V C E K E C
K U R S G P Z R T L O A D E A L R Y
L N H E T M D T R P E I N H T I N R
I D O Y Y L S F U K R T Q P B G A O
R E J W Q A E B T C A H P O L H C L
O L G O L C R Y H E X E U R E T L G
N P V K U E A P Q D T Z X P K V E Y
E I Z J Y B D J K E Y M V H T Z I I
V T S I R H C G R W X L J E S U S L
A L B Z Y O B Y E V I Y N C P Y U H
E U D X T A R U O N O H F A D I A V
H M L O R D A H V Q L F V E H O L Y
J L V W H V S U O I C E R P A G E R
T C P A T I E N C E W X T S U B J Z
```

Peter's Story

2 Peter 1-8

Simon Peter is a servant and an apostle of Jesus Christ to them that have obtained like precious faith with us (him and those who believe) through the righteousness of God and our Savior Jesus Christ. Grace and peace be multiplied to you through the knowledge of God, and of Jesus our Lord. According to His divine power He has given us all things related to life and godliness, through the knowledge of Him that has called us to glory and virtue. Through Him, we have been given exceeding great and precious promises that these might be partakers of the divine nature, having escaped the corruption that is in the world through lust. He has given all diligence. We are to add to our faith virtue; and to virtue knowledge. Then add to knowledge temperance; and to temperance patience; and to patience godliness; and godliness to brotherly kindness; to brotherly kindness charity. For if these things be in you, and abound, they make you that you shall neither be barren nor unfruitful in the knowledge of our Lord Jesus Christ.

2 Peter 1:14, 16-20

Peter called his body a tabernacle. We are to turn away from doing evil with our bodies and to do what is right as Jesus has done. He taught the people about the power of the Lord Jesus Christ and His coming because he was an eyewitness.

Jesus received from God the Father honour and glory, when a voice spoke to him from the excellent glory, "This is my beloved Son, in whom I am well pleased."

This voice came from heaven and he and the other disciples with him heard it on the holy mount. It is a true prophecy. His light shines in a dark place until the dawn, and the day star arise in people's hearts. Prophecy was spoke through men by the power of the Holy Spirit.

WORD SEARCH PUZZLE– Galatians

SECRET WORDS: (They can be obvious)

Abraham	Faith	Jesus	Miracles	Righteous
Believed	Galatians	Justify	Obey	Seed
Blessing	God	Law	Perfect	Spirit
Book	Grace	Live	Preach	Truth
Christ	Given	Made	Redeemed	Voice

```
X  C  S  R  E  T  S  I  N  I  M  B  T  S  U  J  A  M
K  O  E  U  T  R  I  V  H  L  D  N  E  V  I  G  I  Z
Z  F  E  D  A  M  O  Y  I  Y  J  R  F  W  O  R  K  S
P  Y  D  T  U  I  A  V  P  G  V  H  L  B  A  J  Q  P
R  Q  K  M  C  B  E  I  R  A  M  U  E  C  G  O  R  A
B  I  O  E  W  O  N  A  O  L  B  Y  L  Y  K  E  X  C
Z  L  G  D  G  P  C  R  X  A  O  E  D  N  A  L  H  O
J  X  E  H  Y  E  Z  D  M  T  S  A  U  C  T  R  E  K
B  G  O  S  T  K  L  F  U  I  V  N  H  P  I  A  P  D
E  Q  E  V  S  E  A  J  T  A  Z  D  U  S  K  R  V  L
L  D  B  N  L  I  O  Y  E  N  X  M  T  C  O  Q  Z  G
I  H  V  K  T  B  N  U  Q  S  T  F  P  M  W  M  O  Y
E  C  T  J  Y  I  D  G  S  O  U  V  I  D  A  D  J  T
V  D  S  I  R  H  L  J  Y  W  X  S  J  H  Q  U  I  R
E  L  M  Z  A  O  B  E  K  V  E  Y  A  C  K  R  D  U
D  U  A  C  T  F  R  P  S  N  O  R  F  M  I  O  L  T
H  M  Q  W  X  D  A  U  I  Q  B  F  V  P  E  V  O  H
J  Y  L  E  P  S  O  G  Z  A  C  T  S  W  A  G  J  B
T  C  E  F  R  E  P  K  J  Z  D  E  M  E  E  D  E  R
```

Galatians' Story continued...

Galatians 2:16, 20-21

16know that a man is not justified by observing the law, but by faith in Jesus Christ. So we, too, have put our faith in Christ Jesus that we may be justified by faith in Christ and not by observing the law, because by observing the law no one will be justified.

20I have been crucified with Christ and I no longer live, but Christ lives in me. The life I live in the body, I live by faith in the Son of God, who loved me and gave himself for me. 21I do not set aside the grace of God, for if righteousness could be gained through the law, Christ died for nothing!"

Galatians 3:1-14

You foolish Galatians! Who has bewitched you? Before your very eyes Jesus Christ was clearly portrayed as crucified.

2I would like to learn just one thing from you: Did you receive the Spirit by observing the law, or by believing what you heard?

3Are you so foolish? After beginning with the Spirit, are you now trying to attain your goal by human effort?

4Have you suffered so much for nothing-if it really was for nothing?

5Does God give you his Spirit and work miracles among you because you observe the law, or because you believe what you heard?

6Consider Abraham: "He believed God, and it was credited to him as righteousness."

7Understand, then, that those who believe are children of Abraham.

8The Scripture foresaw that God would justify the Gentiles by faith, and announced the gospel in advance to Abraham: "All nations will be blessed through you."

9So those who have faith are blessed along with Abraham, the man of faith.

10All who rely on observing the law are under a curse, for it is written: "Cursed is everyone who does not continue to do everything written in the Book of the Law.

WORD SEARCH PUZZLE– Bezalel and Oholiab

SECRET WORDS: (They can be obvious)

Ahisamach	Embroidery	Lord	Son	Wisdom
Aholiab	Engraver	Moses	Stones	Wise
Ark	Filled	Oil	Tabernacle	Wood
Bezaleel	Gold	Purple	Teach	
Blue	Heart	Sanctuary	Timber	
Brass	Judah	Service	Tribe	
Carving	Knowledge	Scarlet	Uri	
Dan	Linen	Silver	Weaver	

```
Z  T  X  Y  P  E  M  B  R  O  I  D  E  R  Y  O  G  N  U
L  F  A  V  R  O  G  A  H  Q  X  C  Z  T  V  A  Q  R  E
C  R  V  B  W  I  S  D  O  M  I  H  Y  J  P  Y  I  X  V
K  S  G  R  E  A  C  Y  E  V  F  O  K  E  U  B  N  K  S
F  M  J  N  M  R  D  G  R  L  J  D  O  O  W  D  G  T  S
D  K  Z  Q  I  E  N  E  T  B  W  Z  P  A  L  Y  A  P  A
A  V  C  P  L  D  S  A  U  X  I  O  Q  H  B  I  C  H  R
N  H  O  L  I  B  S  N  G  C  E  R  T  N  Y  S  T  O  W  B
Q  F  I  E  W  H  J  A  H  L  L  E  Z  K  H  L  V  L  F
L  F  Z  S  D  E  S  Q  T  Y  E  P  V  S  I  P  U  Z  D
E  X  O  I  A  P  A  N  Z  S  C  G  R  A  W  E  P  L  T
E  U  C  W  Y  M  Z  V  A  J  R  F  B  U  R  V  O  E  Z
L  V  N  D  N  X  A  S  E  M  U  E  V  S  P  G  J  L  B
A  H  Q  J  U  E  G  C  I  R  K  T  D  H  E  D  N  U  T
Z  L  C  T  W  O  N  K  H  L  P  R  F  N  O  S  V  N  R
E  G  U  A  K  Y  L  I  V  K  V  L  O  Z  U  Y  O  A  I
B  W  Q  J  E  X  O  B  L  V  U  E  Y  W  T  V  Z  M  B
R  E  B  M  I  T  R  A  E  H  B  X  R  F  M  W  H  Q  E
S  T  O  N  E  S  D  K  L  Z  W  Q  G  N  I  V  R  A  C
```

Bezalel and Oholiab's Story

Exodus 31:1-11
And the Lord spoke to Moses saying, See I have called by name Bezalel the son of Uri, the son of the tribe of Judah: and I have filled him with the spirit of God, in wisdom, and in understanding, and in knowledge, and all manner of workmanship. the tent of meeting, the ark of the covenant law with the atonement cover on it, and all the other furnishings of the tent— the table and its articles, the pure gold lampstand and all its accessories, the altar of incense, the altar of burnt offering and all its utensils, the basin with its stand— and also the woven garments, both the sacred garments for Aaron the priest and the garments for his sons when they serve as priests, and the anointing oil and fragrant incense for the Holy Place. They are to make them just as I commanded you."

Exodus 35:30-35
Moses called Bezaleel the son of Uri, the son of Hur, of the tribe of Judah; and he had filled him with the spirit of God, in wisdom, in understanding, and in knowledge, and in all manner of workmanship; and to devise curious works, to work in gold, and in silver,
and in brass, and in cutting of stones, to set them, and in carving of wood, to make all manner of cunning work. He has put in his heart that he may teach. Aholiab also has received from God and able to teach. He is from the tribe of Dan. He has been filled with wisdom of heart, to work all manner of work, of the engraver, and of the cunning workman, and of the embroider, in blue, and in purple, in scarlet, and in fine linen, and of the weaver, even of them that do any work, and of those that devise cunning work.

Bezalel and Oholiab's Story continued...

Exodus 36:1-2
Bezalel and Aholiab and every wise hearted man in whose heart the Lord had put wisdom and understanding to know how to work all manner of work for the service as the Lord had commanded. Moses called Bezalel and Aholiab and every wise heart man in whose heart the Lord had put wisdom even those whose heart was stirred up to come to do the work.

Exodus 37
Bezalel made the ark of acacia wood—two and a half cubits long, a cubit and a half wide, and a cubit and a half high. He overlaid it with pure gold, both inside and out, and made a gold molding around it. He cast four gold rings for it and fastened them to its four feet, with two rings on one side and two rings on the other. Then he made poles of acacia wood and overlaid them with gold. And he inserted the poles into the rings on the sides of the ark to carry it.

He made the atonement cover of pure gold—two and a half cubits long and a cubit and a half wide. Then he made two cherubim out of hammered gold at the ends of the cover. He made one cherub on one end and the second cherub on the other; at the two ends he made them of one piece with the cover. The cherubim had their wings spread upward, overshadowing the cover with them. The cherubim faced each other, looking toward the cover.

The Table
They made the table of acacia wood—two cubits long, a cubit wide and a cubit and a half high. Then they overlaid it with pure gold and made a gold molding around it. They also made around it a rim a handbreadth wide and put a gold molding on the rim. They cast four gold rings for the table and fastened them to the four corners, where the four legs were. The rings were put close to the rim to hold the poles used in carrying the table.

Bezalel and Oholiab's Storycontinued...

The poles for carrying the table were made of acacia wood and were overlaid with gold. And they made from pure gold the articles for the table—its plates and dishes and bowls and its pitchers for the pouring out of drink offerings.

The Lampstand

They made the lampstand of pure gold. They hammered out its base and shaft, and made its flowerlike cups, buds and blossoms of one piece with them. Six branches extended from the sides of the lampstand—three on one side and three on the other. Three cups shaped like almond flowers with buds and blossoms were on one branch, three on the next branch and the same for all six branches extending from the lampstand. And on the lampstand were four cups shaped like almond flowers with buds and blossoms. One bud was under the first pair of branches extending from the lampstand, a second bud under the second pair, and a third bud under the third pair—six branches in all. The buds and the branches were all of one piece with the lampstand, hammered out of pure gold.

They made its seven lamps, as well as its wick trimmers and trays, of pure gold. They made the lampstand and all its accessories from one talent of pure gold.

The Altar of Incense

They made the altar of incense out of acacia wood. It was square, a cubit long and a cubit wide and two cubits high—its horns of one piece with it. They overlaid the top and all the sides and the horns with pure gold, and made a gold molding around it. They made two gold rings below the molding—two on each of the opposite sides—to hold the poles used to carry it. They made the poles of acacia wood and overlaid them with gold.

They also made the sacred anointing oil and the pure, fragrant incense—the work of a perfumer.

Bezalel and Oholiab's Story continued...

Exodus 38

They built the altar of burnt offering of acacia wood, three cubits[b] high; it was square, five cubits long and five cubits wide. They made a horn at each of the four corners, so that the horns and the altar were of one piece, and they overlaid the altar with bronze. 3 They made all its utensils of bronze—its pots, shovels, sprinkling bowls, meat forks and firepans. They made a grating for the altar, a bronze network, to be under its ledge, halfway up the altar. They cast bronze rings to hold the poles for the four corners of the bronze grating. They made the poles of acacia wood and overlaid them with bronze. They inserted the poles into the rings so they would be on the sides of the altar for carrying it. They made it hollow, out of boards.

The Basin for Washing

hey made the bronze basin and its bronze stand from the mirrors of the women who served at the entrance to the tent of meeting.

The Courtyard

Next they made the courtyard. The south side was a hundred cubits long and had curtains of finely twisted linen, 10 with twenty posts and twenty bronze bases, and with silver hooks and bands on the posts. The north side was also a hundred cubits long and had twenty posts and twenty bronze bases, with silver hooks and bands on the posts.

The west end was fifty cubits wide and had curtains, with ten posts and ten bases, with silver hooks and bands on the posts. The east end, toward the sunrise, was also fifty cubits wide. Curtains fifteen cubits long were on one side of the entrance, with three posts and three bases, and curtains fifteen cubits long were on the other side of the entrance to the courtyard, with three posts and three bases. All the curtains around the courtyard were of finely twisted linen.

Bezalel and Oholiab's Story continued...

The bases for the posts were bronze. The hooks and bands on the posts were silver, and their tops were overlaid with silver; so all the posts of the courtyard had silver bands.

The curtain for the entrance to the courtyard was made of blue, purple and scarlet yarn and finely twisted linen—the work of an embroiderer. It was twenty cubits long and, like the curtains of the courtyard, five cubits high, with four posts and four bronze bases. Their hooks and bands were silver, and their tops were overlaid with silver. All the tent pegs of the tabernacle and of the surrounding courtyard were bronze.

WORD SEARCH PUZZLE– Enoch

SECRET WORDS: Adam, Convince, Deeds

Comes	God	Judgment	Sixty	Ungodly
Days	Had	King	Sons	Walked
Daughters	Him	Methuselah	Ten	Was
Enoch	Hundred	Prophesied	Thousand	Years
Execute	Lived	Saints	Three	
Five	Lord	Seventh	Took	

```
Z  A  T  Y  A  H  S  E  T  L  Q  M  Y  L  D  O  G  N  U
K  P  X  E  R  O  L  A  H  D  X  S  Z  T  C  A  Q  P  E
C  H  V  A  N  V  D  L  E  Y  R  H  D  U  P  R  Y  S  V
R  I  J  R  H  A  C  I  U  G  F  O  K  E  W  B  N  L  Z
F  M  G  S  M  Z  S  V  H  M  J  X  L  B  E  O  G  T  X
D  E  Z  B  K  E  H  T  L  B  Z  S  A  O  I  D  R  O  A
T  L  C  W  H  G  N  C  F  K  P  T  Q  H  B  Y  M  K  D
N  X  A  P  B  E  F  E  O  V  D  N  H  Y  S  T  C  E  B
Q  F  O  J  M  O  C  H  S  M  G  I  Z  U  H  P  V  F  T
B  R  L  G  S  N  Y  J  F  Y  E  A  R  S  A  I  W  L  H
P  D  D  W  I  R  U  Q  Z  P  C  S  O  W  L  B  P  Z  R
G  U  Z  V  L  D  E  S  A  I  V  F  K  D  E  R  V  M  E
J  A  N  J  Y  X  Z  T  R  N  S  I  V  P  S  Q  J  O  E
V  O  H  Q  E  N  O  C  H  E  N  B  J  H  U  O  Y  L  P
C  L  M  C  T  O  U  M  V  G  P  F  O  C  H  R  N  F  X
W  I  U  N  K  Y  R  E  X  Y  U  Z  I  N  T  Q  D  S  N
H  T  Q  G  X  L  N  B  R  Q  L  A  V  A  E  V  A  Z  T
E  Y  N  B  P  T  H  U  N  D  R  E  D  Y  M  W  H  B  J
J  R  A  Z  H  D  E  K  L  A  W  S  I  X  T  Y  G  R  I
```

Enoch's Story

Genesis 5:21-24
And Enoch lived sixty-five years and had Methusaleh. He walked with God after he had his son, Methusaleh at three hundred years old and he had other sons and daughters. And all the days of Enoch were three hundred sixty-five years. And Enoch walked with God; and he was no more; for God took him.

It is recorded that he pleased God, so that's why God took him away. He didn't die, but he lived with God in heaven. In the book of Revelation, it speaks of two witnesses coming to judge the nations of the world. The only two men that never died in the bible were Elijah and Enoch. Moses had died, but his body was not found. Jesus stood in the midst of Moses and Elijah in Matthew, Mark, Luke, and John.

Jude 14-15
Enoch was the seventh generation from Adam. He prophesied about the Lord coming ten thousand of his saints. God would execute judgment to the ungodly people. In those days, the people did ungodly deeds that made God angry. Enoch tried to convince the people. The ungodly sinners spoke against him with hard speeches.

WORD SEARCH PUZZLE– Proverbs 31 Woman

SECRET WORDS: merchandise, silk, wool

Arise	Fears	Linen	Proverbs	Woman
Blessed	Field	Lord	Rejoice	Virtuous
Bread	Fruit	Makes	Rubies	
Children	Good	Mouth	Seeks	
Delivers	Hands	Needy	Scarlet	
Excel	Honour	Poor	Strength	
Favour	Husband	Praise	Trust	

```
S V E S I A R P M U X P K T I Z L O M
R B M Y H T G D E L I V E R S G Z P A
A K F M S E I B U R H C Z B X U H C K
E Q P W D X K C Z F N T M Q Y D R G E
F H O A U L R T E K A P G H L N Q T S
V O E Y I N B X P W R T V N J I W O B
L R X S F I C M D O I X C P E U N V G
B A M D J E O Y V D S M R G Z R Q E A
H E J N L U Z E B U E H N O A C T L N
U C G A T P R A O R E I Y O H M I S X
S I K H V B L U C N K N F D R P U G D
B O Q F S K T H O H S T L U W J R Q E
A J C M Y R A P L R G Z O C Q B F T S
N E X G I N W Y D E E N Z F M A C I S
D R P V D K C X F V O W L B V L V H E
C T L I Q Y O I N H P A Z O J K O X L
X K S T B R E W M J X K U D I Z T R B
G E W A P L Y H T E L R A C S G F U D
B J V O D N R K G W P F Y N E M O W K
```

74

Proverbs 31 Woman's Story continued...

Proverbs 31:10-31

10 A wife of noble character who can find? She is worth far more than rubies.11 Her husband has full confidence in her and lacks nothing of value.12 She brings him good, not harm, all the days of her life.13 She selects wool and flax and works with eager hands. 14 She is like the merchant ships, bringing her food from afar. 15 She gets up while it is still night; she provides food for her family and portions for her female servants. 16 She considers a field and buys it; out of her earnings she plants a vineyard. 17 She sets about her work vigorously; her arms are strong for her tasks. 18 She sees that her trading is profitable, and her lamp does not go out at night. 19 In her hand she holds the distaff and grasps the spindle with her fingers. 20 She opens her arms to the poor and extends her hands to the needy.

21 When it snows, she has no fear for her household; for all of them are clothed in scarlet. 22 She makes coverings for her bed; she is clothed in fine linen and purple 23 Her husband is respected at the city gate,   where he takes his seat among the elders of the land. 24 She makes linen garments and sells them, and supplies the merchants with sashes. 25 She is clothed with strength and dignity; she can laugh at the days to come. 26 She speaks with wisdom, and faithful instruction is on her tongue. 27 She watches over the affairs of her household and does not eat the bread of idleness. 28 Her children arise and call her blessed; her husband also, and he praises her: 29 "Many women do noble things, but you surpass them all." 30 Charm is deceptive, and beauty is fleeting; but a woman who fears the Lord is to be praised. 31 Honor her for all that her hands have done, and let her works bring her praise at the city gate.

Jesus as the King of Kings
from the Book of Revelation

Chelsea
Kong
Feb 17, 2016

Answers

CROSSWORD PUZZLE – ESTHER ANSWERS

									13W	O	14M	E	N
1E	2S	T	3H	E	R						A		
	H		A						12M		J		
	U		D		11F				O		E		
	S		4A	H	A	S	U	E	R	U	S		
	H		S		S				D		T		
	A		S		T		7K		E		Y		
	N		A				I		C				
			5H	A	6M	A	N		A				
					O		G		I		9V		
					N		D				A		
					T		O				S		
					H		8M	Y	R	R	H		
					S						T		
										10O	I	L	

CROSSWORD PUZZLE – EZEKIEL ANSWERS

			¹I				
	²J	O	S	E	P	H	
			R				
		³V	A	L	L	E	Y
			E				
⁷B		⁴F	L	⁵E	S	H	
O				Z			
N		⁶B	R	E	A	T	H
E				K			
⁸S	P	I	R	I	T		
				E			
				⁹L	O	R	¹⁰D
		¹¹S					R
¹²P	R	O	P	H	E	S	Y
		N					

CROSSWORD PUZZLE – EZRA ANSWERS

			¹P					⁸L					
	²C	Y	R	U	³S			E		¹⁰L			
			I		C			V		O			
			⁴E	Z	R	A		⁹I	S	R	A	E	L
			S		I			T		D			
			T		B			E			¹¹B		
				⁵J	E	R	U	S	A	L	E	M	
				U							N		
⁶B	U	I	L	D				¹²H			J		
				A				E			A		
⁷E	A	R	T	H				A			M		
					¹³G			V			I		
					¹⁴O	F	F	E	R	I	N	G	
					D			N					

CROSSWORD PUZZLE – JACOB ANSWERS

							⁷A					¹³L		
¹P	E	N	²I	E	L	⁸O	B	E	Y	⁹E	D	A		
			S				I			S		B		
			A				M	¹⁰J	A	C	O	¹¹B		
			A	⁴H			E			U	¹²L	A	N	D
	³R	A	C	H	E	L	L					E		
			A	A			E					S		
		⁵L		V			C	¹⁴J	O	S	E	P	H	
	⁶R	E	B	E	K	A	H					E		
		A		N				¹⁵S	O	W	E	D		
		H												

CROSSWORD PUZZLE – SOLOMON ANSWERS

							¹G		³W					
							O		I					
						²B	L	E	S	S	E	D		
							D		D					
			⁷J					⁴L	O					
			E		⁶S	O	L	O	M	O	N			
			R		H			V						
		⁸Q	U	E	E	N		E						
			S		B		⁵D	R	E	A	M			
			A		A									
⁹B	U	I	L	T		¹¹G	L	O	R	Y				
			E			R								
	¹⁰T	E	M	P	L	E								
				¹²A	P	P	E	A	R	E	D			
			T			A								

FILL-IN PUZZLE – DEUTERONOMY BLESSINGS ANSWERS

FIELD
BLESSINGS
HEAVEN
HEARKEN
ABOVE
OVER
LAND
VOICE
BLESSED
WORK
BASKET
WAYS
HOLY
HOUSE
GROUND
HIGH
HEAD
STOREHOUSE
PLENTY
DAY
KINE
NATION
RAIN
GOODS
ESTABLISH

FILL-IN PUZZLE – DAVID ANSWERS

Across/Down answers (filled grid):

DAVID · KING · SERVANT · ARK · ISRAEL · ITTAI · KINGDOM · ZADOK · ABSALOM · NATHAN · PRIESTS · ABIATHAR · BANISHED · HUSHAI · BATHSHEBA · SOLOMON · JORDAN · JOAB · AHITHOPHEL · INHERITANCE · FAIR · AHIMELECH

FILL-IN PUZZLE – PROVERBS 31 ANSWERS

Across/Down answers (filled grid):

PROVERBS · BREAD · REACHES · WOMEN · MOUTH · REJOICE · SPINDLE · LINEN · STRENGTH · FRUIT · EXCELLEST · CHILDREN · HONOUR · WAYS · ARISE · NIGHT · FAVOUR · FIELD · LAND · RUBY · DAY · PRAISE · VIRTUOUS · DELIVERETH · HANDLE · MERCHANDISE

FILL-IN PUZZLE – PROVERBS 31 ANSWERS

```
      M                 R O B B I N G
B R E A K     F         R         L                               P
  O     L A     H I S   F     M E                       F R U I T
  O     A     R     I         S I L V E R     C           R     E
  M     C O V E N A N T     S         S         H         I     M
        H         E         E     K E P T       A         F     P
      T I T H E S O     R         D           U       A   L
      E         S O     R                     R       G S     E   E
  A S K         A L M I G H T Y       A N C E S T O R S
      T         P         O                           A       E
                L                           S E N D       E
              J U D A H                               D       K
```

FILL-IN PUZZLE – REVELATION ANSWERS

```
    L E A V E S       A M E T H Y S T
  L                   L     N           O V E R C O M E S
  I           P R O P H E T S
H E A V E N   U     H     W               B O O K
O         A   R     A     C H R Y S O L Y T E     E
L   T H R O N E               I             R     E
Y       T             V   T     S A R D O N Y X   P
  L I G H T       G L O R Y   A       N   L
  O   O   R           I       P       E
  R   D   E           C     T O P A Z
  D     J E R U S A L E M     H             G A T E
          O           I   R E I G N         O
F O U N D A T I O N       N     R           L A M B
              O M E G A   E M E R A L D
```

SCRAMBLED PUZZLE – ABRAHAM ANSWERS

Abram	Lot
Abraham	Nations
Bless	Plain
Canaan	Pharaoh
Cattle	Prophet
Covenant	Rich
Egypt	Sarai
Faith	Sarah
Give	Seed
God	Tent
Great	Walk
Land	
Lord	

SCRAMBLED PUZZLE – ISAIAH ANSWERS

Dehaa	Gnkis
Genal	Anld
Hzhaa	Eycrm
Lsabt	Edyaper
Lcaen	Vase
Yads	Icsk
Earhd	Uns
Zekehiah	Words
Aihasi	Emit
Audhj	Rstut
Eeramusjle	Iniosv
Dilekld	

SCRAMBLED PUZZLE – JOB ANSWERS

Asses	Lord
Bildad	Perfect
Blessed	Prayed
Boils	Satan
Camels	Seven
Daughters	Servants
Elihu	Sheep
Eliphaz	Sons
Fairest	Three
God	Oxen
Job	Wife
Lived	Zophar

SCRAMBLED PUZZLE – JOEL ANSWERS

Blow	Mountain
Cleanse	Nation
Corn	Oil
Cry	Pethuel
Fast	Strong
Fire	Stars
Joel	Sun
Heaven	Trumpet
Holy	War
Horses	Wine
Lion	Vine
Moon	Zion

SCRAMBLED PUZZLE - HABAKKUK ANSWERS

Eagle	Proud
Eat	Run
Faith	Saw
Fly	See
Great	Soul
Habakkuk	Speak
Just	Stand
Live	Table
March	Tower
Nations	Wait
Plain	Watch
Prophet	Write

WORD MATCH PUZZLE - GIDEON ANSWERS

Altar that Gideon built	Angel
False God the men of Abiezer worshipped	Baal
Gideon's father	Egypt
Gideon's army he brought to Phurah	Gideon
He visited Gideon	Israel
Mighty man of valour	Lord
The children of Israel were brought out of	Midianites
The enemies that the Lord delivered the Israelites	Jehovah-Shalom
The people the Lord brought out of Egypt	Joash
They wanted to kill Gideon	The people of Abiezer
	Three hundred men

WORD MATCH PUZZLE – SAMUEL ANSWERS

Elkanah's wife that had children	Elkanah
He had favour with God and men	Eli
He visited Hannah and she conceived	Gift that Hannah brought to the temple
Linen ephod	Hannah
Place where Elkanah and Hannah live	Hophi and Phinehas
Samuel's father	Lord
She had no children until after she prayed	Peninnah
Sons of Eli	Ramah
The priest that Samuel served	Samuel
Three bullocks, one ephah of flour, and a bottle of wine	Samuel's clothing

WORD MATCH PUZZLE – JESUS ANSWERS

He asked Jesus to call him to walk on water	Disciples
He walked on the water	Faith
He was put in prison by Herod for Herodias	Five loaves and two fishes
Herodias daughter danced before him	Five thousand men
Jesus had this when He walked on water	Herod
Jesus is known to be	Jesus
The disciples found this much leftover	John the Baptist
The disciples gave Jesus to feed the multitude	Peter
They gave the bread and the fishes to Jesus	Son of God
The number of the multitude that heard Jesus	Twelve Baskets

WORD MATCH PUZZLE - JOEL ANSWERS

Blow the trumpet in...
He is gracious and merciful, slow to anger, and of great kindness, and repents him of the evil.
The Lord promised to pour out this over all flesh
He said to proclaim among these people; Prepare war, wake up mighty men of war, draw near; let them come up
I will gather all the nations, and bring them down into the valley of...
Ministers of the Lord
The Lord said to these people, "Sanctify a fast..."
The mountains shall drop down new wine...
This place will dwell in Jerusalem forever

Children of Israel
Gentiles
Jehoshophat
Jerusalem
Joel
Judah
Lord
Priests
Spirit
Zion

WORD MATCH PUZZLE - EPHESIANS ANSWERS

Blow the trumpet in...
He is gracious and merciful, slow to anger, and of great kindness, and repents him of the evil.
The Lord promised to pour out this over all flesh
He said to proclaim among these people, Prepare War, wake up mighty men of war, draw near; let them come up
I will gather all the nations, and bring them down into the valley of...
Ministers of the Lord
The Lord said to these people, "Sanctify a fast..."
The mountains shall drop down new wine...
This place will dwell in Jerusalem forever

Children of Israel
Gentiles
Jehoshophat
Jerusalem
Joel
Judah
Lord
Priests
Spirit
Zion

WORD SEARCH PUZZLE – PETER ANSWERS

```
E  C  N  A  D  N  U  B  A  M  J  Y  T  S  E  J  A  M
K  O  E  U  T  R  I  V  H  L  D  N  O  A  U  Z  V  R
N  W  G  J  F  R  O  Y  E  I  N  R  E  W  O  P  T  Q
A  Y  R  Q  M  I  A  P  V  C  B  Q  L  X  G  D  A  P
B  P  T  B  C  B  S  I  Z  L  M  H  P  Y  R  O  B  A
M  S  O  E  V  O  N  X  O  A  G  F  V  C  E  K  E  C
K  U  R  S  G  P  Z  R  T  L  O  A  D  E  A  L  R  Y
L  N  H  E  T  M  D  T  R  P  E  I  N  H  T  I  N  R
I  D  O  Y  Y  L  S  F  U  K  R  T  Q  P  B  G  A  O
R  E  J  W  Q  A  E  B  T  C  A  H  P  O  L  H  C  L
O  L  G  O  L  C  R  Y  H  E  X  E  U  R  E  T  L  G
N  P  V  K  U  E  A  P  Q  D  T  Z  X  P  K  V  E  Y
E  I  Z  J  Y  B  D  J  K  E  Y  M  V  H  T  Z  I  I
V  T  S  I  R  H  C  G  R  W  X  L  J  E  S  U  S  L
A  L  B  Z  Y  O  B  Y  E  V  I  Y  N  C  P  Y  U  H
E  U  D  X  T  A  R  U  O  N  O  H  F  A  D  I  A  V
H  M  L  O  R  D  A  H  V  Q  L  F  V  E  H  O  L  Y
J  L  V  W  H  V  S  U  O  I  C  E  R  P  A  G  E  R
T  C  P  A  T  I  E  N  C  E  W  X  T  S  U  B  J  Z
```

WORD SEARCH PUZZLE – GALATIANS
ANSWERS

```
X C S R E T S I N I M B T S U J A M
K O E U T R I V H L D N E V I G I M
Z F E D A M O Y I Y J R F W O R K Z
P Y D T U I A V P G V H L B A J Q S
R Q K M C B E I R A M U E C G O R P
B I O E W O N A O L M B Y Y K E X A
Z L G D G P C Z X A I O E N A L H O
J X E H Y E Z D M T V B A C T I R K
B G O Y T K L F U I V Z N M I K A D
E Q E S E A A J I A S X M H S O Q V
L D E N S L O Y E N T M U P C W M Z
I H V K T B N U Q S F P I W A M W O
E C T J Y I O D G S O U S D J H Q J
V D S M R L G J Y W X V E Y A C K U
E L M Z A O B E K V E Y R F M I O I
D U A C T R P S N O R F V C M P E O
H M Q W X D A U I Q B F V P W I E V
J Y L E P S O G Z A C T S E A A G J
T C E F R E P K J Z D E M E E D E R
```

WORD SEARCH PUZZLE – BEZALEEL & OHOLIAB ANSWERS

```
Z T X Y P E M B R O I D E R Y O G N U
L F A V R O G A H Q X C Z T V A Q R E
C R V B W I S D O M I H Y J P Y I X V
K S G R E A C Y E V F O K E U B N K S
F M J N M R D G R L J D O O W D G T D
D K Z Q I E N E T B W Z P A L Y A P A
A V C P L D S A U X I O Q H B I C H R
N H O L I B N G C E R T N Y S T O W B
Q F I E W H J A H L L E Z K H L V L F
L F Z S D E S Q T Y E P V S I P U Z D
E X O I A P A N Z S C G R A W E P L T
E U C W Y M Z V A J R F B U R V O E Z
L V N D N X A S E M U E V S P G J L B
A H Q J U E G C I R K T D H E D N U T
Z L C T W O N K H L P R F N O S V N R
E G U A K Y L I V K V L O Z U Y O A I
B W Q J E X O B L V U E Y W T V Z M B
R E B M I T R A E H B X R F M W H Q E
S T O N E S D K L Z W Q G N I V R A C
```

```
Z A T Y A H S E T L Q M Y L D O G N U
K P X E R O L A H D X S Z T C A Q P E
C H V A N V D L E Y R H D U P R B S V
R I J R H A C I U G F O L E W B N L Z
F M G S M Z S V M J X L B E O G T X
D E Z B K E H T B Z S A O D R M K A D
T L C W H G N C K P T Q H B Y T C E B
N X A P B E F E O V D N H Y P V E F B
Q F O J M O C H S M G I Z S A I W L T
B R L G S R Y J F Y C S O W L B P Z H
P D D W I D U Q Z P C S K D E R V M E
G U Z V Y E S A I V F K V P S Q J O E
J A N J Y X Z T R N S I V P S Q J L P
V O H Q E N O C H E N B J H U O Y F X
C L M C T O M V G P F O C H R N F X
W I U N K Y R E X Y U Z I N T Q D S N
H T Q G X L N B R Q L A V A E V A Z T
E Y N B P T H U N D R E D Y M W H B J
J R A Z H D E K L A W S I X T Y G R I
```

WORD SEARCH PUZZLE – PROVERBS 31
ANSWERS

```
S  V  E  S  I  A  R  P  M  U  X  P  K  T  I  Z  L  O  M
R  B  M  Y  H  T  G  D  E  L  I  V  E  R  S  G  Z  P  A
A  K  F  M  S  E  I  B  U  R  H  C  Z  B  X  U  H  C  K
E  Q  P  W  D  X  K  C  Z  F  N  T  M  Q  Y  D  R  G  E
F  H  O  A  U  L  R  T  E  K  A  P  G  H  L  N  Q  T  S
V  O  E  Y  J  N  B  X  P  W  R  T  V  N  J  I  W  O  B
L  R  X  S  F  I  C  M  D  O  I  X  C  P  E  U  N  V  G
B  A  M  D  J  E  O  Y  V  D  S  M  R  G  Z  R  Q  E  A
H  E  J  N  L  U  Z  E  B  U  E  H  N  O  A  C  T  L  N
U  C  G  A  T  P  R  A  O  R  E  I  Y  O  H  M  I  S  X
S  I  K  H  V  B  L  U  C  N  K  N  F  D  R  P  U  G  D
B  O  Q  F  S  K  T  H  O  H  S  T  L  U  W  J  R  Q  E
A  J  C  M  Y  R  A  P  L  R  G  Z  O  C  Q  B  F  T  S
N  E  X  G  I  N  W  Y  D  E  E  N  Z  F  M  A  C  I  S
D  R  P  V  D  K  C  X  F  V  O  W  L  B  V  L  V  H  E
C  T  L  I  Q  Y  O  I  N  H  P  A  Z  O  J  K  O  X  L
X  K  S  T  B  R  E  W  M  J  X  K  U  D  I  Z  T  R  B
G  E  W  A  P  L  Y  H  T  E  L  R  A  C  S  G  F  U  B
B  J  V  O  D  N  R  K  G  W  P  F  Y  N  E  M  O  W  K
```

Salvation Prayer

Dear God, I know that I am a sinner. I believe that Jesus Christ died on the cross to pay for my sins and that He rose from the grave after 3 days. That through Him I can have eternal life. I surrender myself to you and ask Jesus Christ to come into my heart to be my Personal Lord and Savior. I receive your eternal life and choose to live for you. I am willing to yield myself to you and let you work in me. Cleanse me with the blood of Jesus Christ. Teach and lead my steps. Deliver me from all sins, transgressions, iniquities, curses, and bondage. Fill me up. Baptize me with the Holy Spirit and with fire in Jesus' name. Amen.

Holy Spirit Baptism Prayer

Holy Spirit, I welcome you to come into my life. Jesus, I believe that you are the Baptizer. Please baptize me with your Holy Spirit and with fire for your glory in Jesus' name. Arrest my tongue to speak for you in Jesus' name to release out the words you want to impart to me in Jesus' name. Amen.

Open your mouth and let the words come out that God gives you. It will be words that you don't know what they mean. You can ask God what it means. You need to let Him talk through you every day to grow this gift.

He will bring you closer to God and you will know Jesus more. You will have power from God to do great things and know things.

Prayer

Thank you Father, open my heart to understand the Bible. Help me to know and receive your word. Teach me what it means and how to live by it every day. I want to do great things for you and love you with my whole heart. Help me Holy Spirit to walk in God's ways and to share it with others in Jesus name. Give me wisdom and the best life you want for me in Jesus name. Amen.

Message from the Author

The children's books focus on teaching children biblical principles for live a godly, God fearing, and successful life. They are best accompanied with the Bible. Her puzzle books teach youth about the Bible capturing passages to accompany with each puzzle. Each of the books is full of 5 types of puzzles making fun to learn. Young children can do these puzzles with the help of an adult. You can also find additional puzzle books on Barnes and Noble for youger children. Teaching the Bible brings transformation to our lives. It gives us answers to the problems we face. We need the Bible in these last days more than before. Ask the Holy Spirit to help you understand what they mean and to apply them to your life every day.

Other Products

The Bridal Collection
Knowing God
How to Hear God's Voice
New Life in Jesus
Loving Israel
God's Gifts
Meeting God
Word Power
Fruit of the Spirit
The Tabernacle
Bride for Jesus
A Life of Prayer
Live Free
Who am I in Jesus
Walk in Love
God's Favor
Man of God
Woman of God
How to Use Money
God's Wisdom
Fasting
See Jerusalem and Bethany
First Fruit Offering
Pentecost
Feast of Trumpets
Day of Atonement
Feast of Tabernacles
Counting the Omer
Festival of Lights
Glory, Presence, and Holy Spirit
Live in God's Presence

31 Day Devotional
Biblical Puzzle Book Vol 1
Biblical Puzzle Book Vol 2
Biblical Puzzle Book Vol 4
Biblical Puzzle Book Vol 5
Biblical Puzzles for Young
Children Book 1
Biblical Puzzles for Young
Children Book 2
Biblical Puzzles for Young
Children Book 3

Teaching Series & Guides
How to Hear God's Voice Teaching Guide
Knowing God, Jesus, and Holy Spirit
Relationship with God, Jesus,
Holy Spirit Guide

Teaching (Non-Sale)
Purim
Passover
Resurrection

And much more!

Please check Chelsea's website for links to other books and products found on Amazon, Barnes and Noble, and Kobo. Please leave a review to help the author to write more books. Thank you!

https://chelseak532002550.wordpress.com

If you are interested in getting other products, please contact:
kayunkk@gmail.com

Coaching Products

Teaching Series Packages to train you to equip you for God's purpose!

Check the website for details:
https://chelseak532002550.wordpress.com

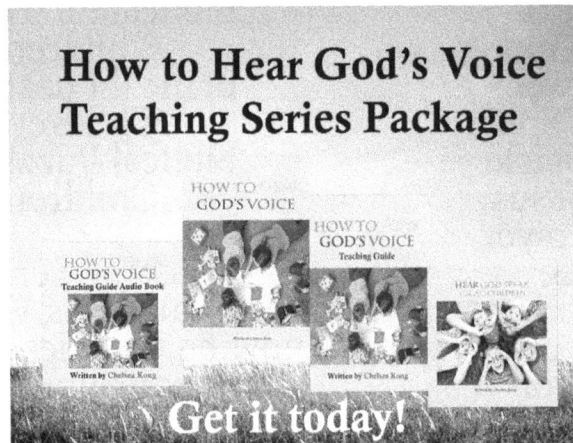

How to Hear God's Voice Teaching Series Package

Get it today!

Complete Knowing Teaching Series

Get it today!

Relationship with God, Jesus, & Holy Spirit Teaching Series Package

Buy yours today!

Learn How to Hear God's Voice
Knowing Him
Build a Relationship with Him

Each package includes lessons and related books

Biography

She is a writer, creative arts and digital media artist, skilled administration professional, and podcaster. Chelsea also served in a variety of roles, from audio-visual, photography, to assisting on the worship team, and ministry team. She also has a passion for families being united.

Chelsea has been a guest on Unity Live Radio and The Lady Tracey Show and is highly recommended by a Proud Christian blog. She graduated from Hotel and Restaurant Management, Digital Media Arts, Office Administration, and experience working with children. Chelsea lives in Toronto, Canada. She mainly writes children's books, stories, bridal writing, poems, lyrics for songs, words of encouragement, blessings, prayers, and jokes. The author of How to Hear the Voice of God, the Bridal Collection, Knowing God, etc. She also has her own Bible Puzzle books and other inspired products. Her podcast channel is called Chelsea K on Anchor, Spotify, and iTunes.

Please check my website to find out more:
https://chelseak532002550.wordpress.com/

Get all 5 Puzzle Books!

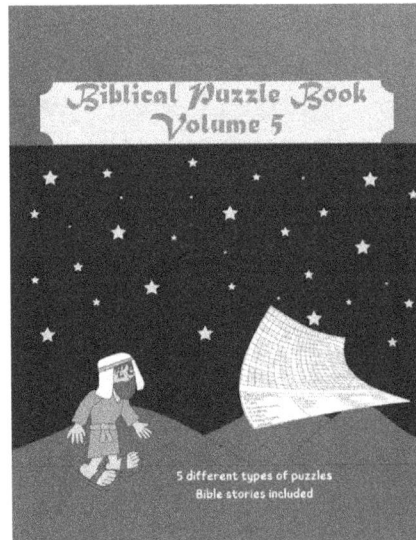

Get the first 2 on Amazon and the last 3 on Barnes and Noble!

www.ingramcontent.com/pod-product-compliance
Lightning Source LLC
Chambersburg PA
CBHW081551040426
42448CB00016B/3287